TABLE OF CONTENTS

Page

ACRONYMS

BG	Brigadier General
CENTCOM	Central Command
COL	Colonel
CPT	Captain
GEN	General
L&N	Louisville and Nashville Railroad
LT	Lieutenant
LTC	Lieutenant Colonel
LTG	Lieutenant General
MAJ	Major
MG	Major General
N&C	Nashville and Chattanooga Railroad
RPG	Rocket-Propelled Grenade
TSC	Theater Support Command

ILLUSTRATIONS

TABLES

CHAPTER 1

INTRODUCTION

> Too often in military history one is disposed to follow in close detail the movements of corps and divisions and companies on the battlefield without inquiring how they got there. Great armies appear, full-blown, from nowhere, do battle, then disappear. If they are to be brought to life, we must see how they live.[1]
>
> James A. Huston

Military operations and logistics are inextricably linked. The ability to transport, feed, arm, and fuel an army in the field is what enables a commander to conduct the strategic, operational, and tactical tasks necessary to fight the nation's wars. Very often it is not the combat forces that decide the outcome of a campaign or battle, rather it is the logistical system that supports the field armies that plays the decisive role because, "supply is the basis of strategy and tactics."[2]

Logistics is defined as "the practical art of moving armies and keeping them supplied"[3] or "that branch of administration which embraces the management and provision of supply, evacuation and hospitalization, transportation and service. It envisages getting the right people and appropriate supplies to the right place at the right time and in the proper condition."[4] The ability to concentrate ammunition, food, transportation, manpower, and others at a specific place and time is what enables commanders to overwhelm and defeat their enemies. Logistics is what makes that possible or impossible.

> Before a commander can even start thinking of maneuvering or giving battle, of marching this way and that, of penetrating, enveloping, encircling, of annihilating or wearing down, in short of putting into practice the whole rigamarole of strategy, he has--or ought--to make sure of his ability to supply his soldiers with those 3,000 calories a day without which they will very soon cease to be of any

> use as soldiers; that roads to carry them to the right place at the right time are available, and that movement along these roads will not be impeded by either a shortage or a superabundance of transportation.[5]

Logistics is what enables an army to sustain itself during combat operations. This was true in the days of the Roman Empire, the Crusades, Napoleon, and the American Civil War and is still true today as shown in Operation Iraqi Freedom. As Karl von Clausewitz wrote, "The system of subsistence will control the war."[6] The concerns that Alexander the Great had during his campaigns 1300 years ago were the same problems Major General (MG) Rosecrans would deal with in 1863: amount of grain needed for horses and mules, number of wagons to be allowed in the army, how far to travel away from the supply depot, how much food can be carried by the supply trains and soldiers and how much to allow to be foraged from the countryside, how many tents to bring, number of ambulances to allow, and others.[7] The technology used in war has changed, but the limitations and possibilities of logistics have generally not changed in thousands of years. As Lieutenant General William G. Pagonis, the senior US logistician in the theater during the Gulf War of 1990-1991, said of this rarely studied aspect of the military, "Logistics is traditionally an unglamorous and underappreciated activity. To generalize, when the battle is going well, the strategist and tactician are lionized; it is only when the tanks run out of gas that people go head-hunting for the logisticians."[8]

Excellent examples of the importance of logistics in campaigns are the Tullahoma and Chickamauga campaigns of the Union Army of the Cumberland during the Civil War. MG William S. Rosecrans had to plan campaigns that drove deep into enemy territory. His ability to equip, feed, and move his 67,000-man force was a much greater worry for him than how it would perform in combat. He had to rely on a tenuous rail link back to Louisville, Kentucky, to support his force as it drove toward Chattanooga, Tennessee, and the Confederate Army of Tennessee, commanded by General Braxton Bragg.

History's timeless lessons give us the perspective and insight to judge ideas, policies, and procedures more thoroughly. The lessons of 140 years ago are valuable to military commanders and planners of today in that they can provide a guide for planning future operations. Through an analysis of the logistical operations of the Army of the Cumberland, a greater understanding of the important role that logistics plays in successful campaigns can be discovered. The challenges that the Army of the Cumberland had to overcome in 1863 are very similar to the challenges faced by commanders in 2005.

Primary Research Question

What can the Army leadership of 2005 learn from the leadership of the Army of the Cumberland in 1863 in the field of logistics and its effect on strategy and tactics?

Secondary Questions

How was the logistical system organized in the Army of the Cumberland, the Department of the Cumberland, and the US Army as a whole in 1863?

1. How was logistical planning conducted?

2. How was the logistical support provided in the Tullahoma and Chickamauga Campaigns?

3. What were key factors that enabled logistics to be a success for MG Rosecrans?

4. What role did rivers, roads, and railroads have in the campaigns?

5. Did the size of the "logistical tail" strengthen or hamper the army?

6. What restrictions did the logistical lines place on MG Rosecrans' planning?

7. Did MG Rosecrans make good use of the time he spent in resupplying his forces and making logistical preparations for the coming campaigns?

Background

The branches of the Army that handled the logistics during the Civil War are essentially the same as today, with minor differences. The Quartermasters were responsible for supplying personal equipment and clothing, tents, horses, mules, food for horses and mules, wagons, medical supplies, and transportation (to include evacuation of the sick and wounded). The Commissary officers supplied all food for human consumption. Medical directors (physicians) operated field and fixed facility hospitals, planned the medical support, ordered medical supplies, treated the sick and wounded, and supervised military and civilian nurses and hospital stewards. Ordnance officers were responsible for obtaining weapons and ammunition for all caliber of weapons (both crew served and personal) and transporting the ammunition to the soldiers. The role of the Engineer officers in rebuilding railroads and bridges because of their large impact on logistical performance will also be explored.

The goal of the logistics system in the military is "to support the soldier in the field with what is needed, where and in the condition and quantity required, at a minimum expenditure of resources."[9] In today's military these are made possible under a concept called Combat Service Support (CSS). Its intent is to allow commanders to "generate combat power, extend operational reach, and sustain the force."[10]

The characteristics of CSS are anticipation of the army's needs, integration of logistical assets in field units, continuity of logistical support, responsiveness to commanders and the soldiers' needs, and improvisation in order to adapt to changing situations.[11] While not written as doctrine in the Civil War, these same characteristics can be used to evaluate the logisticians' performance during Tullahoma and Chickamauga.

In early November 1862, newly promoted Major General William S. Rosecrans arrived in Kentucky to take charge of the recently created Department of the Cumberland which included a part of the old Department of the Ohio under Major General Don Carlos Buell. The army he would create, the Army of the Cumberland, was composed of three wings: the Right Wing under Major General Alexander McCook (the future XX corps), the Center Wing under Major General George H. Thomas (the future XIV corps), and the Left Wing under Major General Thomas L. Crittenden (the future XXI corps). The army was scattered throughout Kentucky and Tennessee with Nashville as its forward position.[12]

Rosecrans was chosen for this new command because of his proven generalship in western Virginia and Mississippi. Abraham Lincoln and the Republican Congress had just taken serious losses in the congressional elections which displayed the countries growing dissatisfaction with the course of the war. Lincoln needed victories to restore his support and MG Buell was accused of having the "slows," unwilling or unable to prosecute an offensive war, so he was replaced. From the day he arrived to his command, Rosecrans was consistently pushed by the government in Washington to use Nashville as a base and from there drive the Confederate forces out of middle and eastern Tennessee. Rosecrans quickly consolidated his forces around Nashville, but once he arrived, he realized his new army was not properly supplied or equipped to conduct offensive operations, especially in the winter. The six weeks following his appointment were spent bringing in supplies from the depots in Bowling Green and Louisville, Kentucky. One of his major concerns was his lack of cavalry. The Confederate cavalry outnumbered his own and they possessed superior leaders. With this force, the Confederates continually raided and destroyed the railroad link back to Kentucky. Despite this, Rosecrans still managed to gather twenty days of supplies in his Nashville warehouses. He was threatened continually from Washington to either march south and confront the Confederates near Murfreesboro or face being relieved. His opportunity came once he had accumulated enough supplies and Confederate General Braxton Bragg had detached the cavalry raiding parties under Brigadier Generals John Hunt Morgan and Nathan Bedford Forrest to Kentucky and west Tennessee, respectively.[13]

The bloody battle at Murfreesboro from 31 December 1862 to 2 January 1863 was a Union defensive victory. Following this bloody battle, the Union Army wintered around Murfreesboro and the Confederates around Tullahoma. MG Rosecrans spent the next six months reorganizing and building up the logistical capabilities of his command. His study of the geography between Murfreesboro and Chattanooga, Tennessee, and the conclusions he drew had significant implications on the Tullahoma and Chickamauga campaigns the following summer. First, moving his army through Tennessee's mountain ranges and river valleys would be difficult in even the best weather conditions. He could not rely on the rivers of the region or the road network to resupply the needs of his men and horses; he had to rely on the Louisville & Nashville and the Nashville & Chattanooga railroads to fill this role. Second, he had to have a better-led and better-equipped cavalry force. Without it, his supply wagons and railroads would always be vulnerable to Confederate cavalry raids. Third, he would not allow the politicians and armchair generals in Washington to push him into battle before he felt his army was absolutely ready with supplies and equipment.[14] These beliefs drove the preparations for the upcoming Tullahoma and Chickamauga campaigns in the summer and fall of 1863.

MG Rosecrans and his staff created a force and a logistical system in the Department of the Cumberland that enabled MG Rosecrans to clear middle Tennessee of Confederate forces and that allow him to capture Chattanooga in September 1863. The need for this vast system also limited his options and his ability to react quickly during these campaigns; it made these victories more difficult to achieve. The strategic, operational, and tactical possibilities for the Army of the Cumberland, like all armies, were being driven by its logistics.

---

[1]James A. Huston, *The Sinews of War: Army Logistics, 1775-1953* (Washington, DC: Office of the Chief of Military History, 1966), ix.

[2]Department of the Army, Field Manual 4-0, *Combat Service Support* (Washington, DC: Department of the Army, August 2003), 1-1 9 (hereafter cited as Field Manual 4-0); and Donald W. Engels, *Alexander the Great and the Logistics of the Macedonian Army* (Berkeley and Los Angeles, California: University of California Press, 1978), 2.

[3]Martin Van Creveld, *Supplying War* (Cambridge, United Kingdom: Cambridge University Press, 1977), 1.

[4]Huston, vii-viii.

[5]Ibid, 1.

[6]Charles R. Schrader, *United States Army Logistics, 1775-1992: An Anthology,* vol. 1 (Honolulu, Hawaii: University Press of the Pacific, 2001), 34.

[7]Engels, 14-18.

[8]William G. Pagonis, *Moving Mountains: Lessons in Leadership and Logistics from the Gulf War* (Boston, Massachusetts: Harvard Business School Press, 1992), x.

[9]Schrader, 29.

[10]Field Manual 4-0, 5-1.

[11]Ibid., 1-2.

[12]Wiliam M. Lamers, *The Edge of Glory: A Biography of General William S. Rosecrans, U.S.A.* (Baton Rouge, Louisiana: Louisiana State University Press, 1999), 181-184.

[13]Ibid., 195-199.

[14]Ibid., 246-252, 264-265.

CHAPTER 2

ORGANIZATION OF THE UNION ARMY LOGISTICAL SYSTEM

> Behind all combat organization and all modern strategy lies a nation's capacity to produce and provide the weapons of war.[1]
>
> Charles R. Schrader

When the Civil War began in 1861, the northern states had numerous advantages over the southern states when it came to creating and supporting armies. Their first advantage was in population. The total Southern population was 9 million, of which 3 ½ million were slaves, and only 1,140,000 were white males between the ages of 15 and 40. The Northern population was 20 million, of which 4,070,000 were white males between ages 15 and 40.[2] The North had 99,564 manufacturing establishments that employed 1,300,000 workers while the South had 16,896 manufacturing establishments employing just 110,000 people,[3] making the South's total share of national manufacturing only 16 percent. The city of Lowell, Massachusetts, operated more textile spindles than all eleven of the Confederate states combined.[4]

Throughout the 1840s and 1850s, there was an ever-rising demand for Southern cotton, hemp, rice, sugar, and tobacco making those crops more and more valuable. Southerners put every available acre into producing those staples for exportation. The production of food crops in the South declined creating a food-deficit region.[5] This was certainly not the case in the northern states where food crops were the money crops for farmers. Michigan, a young state that was only partially cleared of its vast hardwood and pine forests, was already able to produce 5.7 million bushels of corn, nearly 5 million bushels of wheat, and 1.8 bushels of oats, and 90,000 sheep by 1854.[6]

In the field of transportation, the South possessed 9,000 miles of railroads while the North had 20,000.[7] Nearly all the vessels that shipped goods on the rivers and from the ports of South were built and owned by Northern or British companies.[8]

The South also had a problem with producing capital for investment. Most of the South's wealth was tied up in land and slaves; cash for diversified investment was difficult to come by. For example, 7/8ths of the banking in Mobile, Alabama, was owned and controlled by Northerners in 1847.[9] The ability to raise capital, for industry or for war, was not an issue in the North with its great banking houses in New York and Philadelphia.

William T. Sherman summed up the Northern advantage while talking to a Southern friend in 1861, saying;

> The North can make a steam engine, locomotive or railway car; hardly a yard of cloth or a pair of shoes can you make. You are rushing to war with one of the most powerful, ingeniously mechanical and determined people on earth--right at your doors. You are bound to fail. Only in your spirit and determination are you prepared for war. In all else you are totally unprepared.[10]

While the North had tremendous advantages over the South, the difficulty was marshalling those resources in an effective way to overwhelm the Southern Confederacy. Only by creating a bureaucratic machinery that was able to obtain and track funds, build camps, buy equipment and armaments, train officers and men, obtain food and forage, move tens of thousands of men over vast distances, and bring all of these resources to a decisive place at a decisive time could the North win the Civil War. The machinery that accomplished this was headquartered in the War Department in Washington, D.C.

Logistics in the Civil War was controlled by the bureaus or staff departments (the terms were interchangeable[11]) of the War Department. The bureaus had been formed to meet the crisis of the War of 1812. By 1812, the War Department had been downsized to just the Secretary and eight clerks. In response to the expansion of the war effort, Congress created the bureaus to organize the supplying and administration of the armies. The Quartermaster, Ordnance, and Engineer Departments were created in 1812 and the Medical Department in 1813. No Commissary Department for Subsistence was created, this work was done by the Quartermaster Department through contractors. A Commissary General of Purchases was the primary agent for procurement; the bureaus were only the agents for distribution.[12] In 1818, Secretary of War John C. Calhoun drafted a bill that Congress passed creating a separate Subsistence Department. The Ordnance Department was merged with the Artillery branch in 1821 but was restored as a separate bureau in 1832.[13] When the Purchasing Department was virtually abolished in 1842, the bureau chiefs had complete charge of procurement and distribution for their departments.[14] This organization of the supply bureaus would be maintained through the Mexican and Civil Wars.

The power that the bureau chiefs (they held the rank of either colonel or brigadier general) could wield was substantial. This stemmed from two aspects of the War Departments organization--lack of any mandatory retirement age and the fact that the bureau chiefs answered to the civilian leadership (Secretary of War) and not the Army uniformed leadership. The eight bureaus of the War Department--adjutant general, pay, topographical engineers, engineers, quartermaster, subsistence, medical, and ordnance--were often led by officers who had held their bureau chief positions for decades. During Jefferson Davis' tenure as Secretary of War from 1853 to1857, two of the bureau chiefs had held their positions since 1818. This led to the chiefs having tremendous bureaucratic and political power.[15] The position of General-in-Chief was not a legal position with clearly defined responsibilities, but one created within the War Department for the senior general in the army. As the position developed under Brevet Lieutenant General Winfield Scott, who assumed the post in 1841 and held it until 1861, the General-in-Chief only took orders from the President. The Secretary of War had little contact with the General-in-Chief and allowed the General-in-Chief to have no direct influence over the bureaus of the War Department.[16] This was the structure when the Civil War began--the Secretary of War and his bureaus handling the administrative and supply business of the Army and the General-in-Chief directing the line forces in the field.[17] While the two groups understood they needed each other to achieve victory, the system was also very dependent on the compatibility of individual personalities in order to function properly.

The Regular Army of the United States consisted of only 1,108 officers and 15,259 men in 1861. The Army was scattered throughout six geographical departments: East, West, Texas, New Mexico, Utah, and Pacific. These military departments were the basic organizational unit for logistics, and the commander of each department was held responsible for his own logistical support with no intervening levels between his headquarters and the bureaus in Washington. This continued through the Civil War.[18] The 16,000-man Army of 1861 became over 1,000,000 in 1865 and the $22,981,000 in expenditures in 1861 became $1,031,323,000 in 1865. By 1863, the war was costing over $2,000,000 a day.[19] The bureaus were only staffed to support the small frontier force; they had to be greatly expanded when the war began to accomplish the expenditure of these vast sums of money and to track the equipment and services it purchased. For example, the Quartermaster Department went from 13 clerks in 1861 to 591 in 1865.[20]

There was little coordinated planning that occurred either between the bureaus or between the bureaus and military departments. In the spring of 1862, Lincoln and the new Secretary of War Edwin M. Stanton, set up an "Army Board" that consisted of the heads of all the bureaus and chaired by MG Ethan Allen Hitchcock to bring order to the logistics planning for the campaigns to take place that summer. There was little in the way of coordinated long-term planning that took place; each bureau took care of their own responsibilities and made staff estimates without consulting with the other bureaus.[21] This did improve in March 1864 when Ulysses Grant was promoted to lieutenant general and made General-in-Chief. Grant made the previous General-in-Chief, MG Henry Halleck, the Chief of Staff of the Army with the authority to coordinate the bureau operations.[22] The bureaus were required to provide the Secretary of War their estimates for the upcoming fiscal year by 1 October of each year. This assisted with the congressional appropriations process and helped provide a baseline of supplies with which military leaders could make plans for future operations. The estimates were compiled from the reports of the military department commanders filed with the Adjutant General and the prescribed allowances per soldier, animal, and unit by Army regulations.[23]

While the military department commanders were responsible for logistics in their departments and armies, the bureaus in Washington appointed the logistics officers on their staffs. Army, corps, division, and brigade quartermaster, ordnance, commissary, and medical officers were all appointed and assigned to their positions in each military department by their respective bureau chief in Washington, and they held a Regular Army commission with a technical title of , for example, "assistant quartermaster general." (The supply officers each had to post a "bond," usually for $10,000, as a guarantee against fraud by the officer. If fraud was discovered, the money in the bond would be taken by the War Department in partial payment for their losses.)[24] Regiments had a single logistics officer, called the quartermaster, with quartermaster, ordnance, and commissary sergeants that worked for them. The regimental quartermasters were appointed when the volunteer regiments were raised in their home states by the governors of each state.[25] There was a chronic shortage of Regular Army logistics officers throughout the war and volunteer officers were frequently promoted into staff positions in higher organizations. With this chain of command structure, logistics officers were often subject to the orders of army commanders, the senior logistics officer of their bureau in that army, the local depot logistics officer, the regional depot logistics officer, and the bureau chief back in Washington.[26] While the bureau chiefs in Washington sought to have ranks match up with levels of responsibility throughout the units of the armies (example would be colonel at army level, lieutenant colonel at corps, major at division, captain at brigade, lieutenant at regimental), this was not put into place until the last year of the war. Instead, captains could be found running logistics from brigades through armies and contracting for and managing millions of dollars in goods and services.[27] It must also be understood that there were no logistical units at this time that specialized in receiving, storing, and distributing supplies. A small number of logistical staff officers, with a limited number of logistical sergeants, at depot, army, corps, division, and brigade levels, would have soldiers from combat units detailed to assist them and a large number of civilian contract clerks and laborers working under them.[28] This was the way supplies were distributed throughout the Civil War in all the departments.

The War Department established large general depots throughout the North where contracted and government-manufactured goods of all the bureaus could be gathered. Examples are New York, Boston, Philadelphia, Washington, Cincinnati, St. Louis, and Chicago. The department commanders would then set up their main supply depot that would collect the supplies for the field units under their command. For the Department of the Cumberland this was in Louisville, Kentucky. Then, forward logistics bases would be established as distribution sites to the units.[29] Examples for the Army of the Cumberland are Nashville and Murfreesboro, Tennessee, and Stevenson, Alabama.

Since the government factories and arsenals could not provide all the materiel needed for the expanding army, contracts were let with manufacturers for these goods. This was done in a haphazard manner in the opening months of the war. Secretary of War Simon Cameron, the political boss of Pennsylvania, was not experienced at running an organization like the War Department, and he used the offices under his control to enrich his friends. In one incident, Cameron entrusted a political ally named Alexander Cummings, the publisher of the *Philadelphia Bulletin,* with $2,000,000 to purchase supplies. Cummings made numerous verbal contracts for goods, made no requirement for inspection upon delivery, and wasted most of the money entrusted to him, to include $160,000 that ended up in his personal bank account.[30] Cameron's inability to take control of the contracts being let in the department led Lincoln to bypass Cameron and direct Secretary of the Treasury Salmon P. Chase to advanced $2,000,000 to a group of New York business men to purchase military supplies.[31]

With the Federal government in competition with private individuals and state governments for scarce military equipment and arms in the early months of the war, logistical support to the gathering armies was inconsistent and disorganized. When Congress came into special session in July 1861, it was already suspicious of waste and fraud taking place in military procurement. The House of Representatives formed the Select Committee on Government Contracts with oversight on the contracting matters.[32] The committee sought to better control dishonest contracting officers and contractors by making the only legal government contract ones that were in writing and were filed with the Department of the Interior. Quartermaster General Montgomery C. Meigs felt this would not only put a stranglehold on the procurement process but was also not an effective deterrent for fraud. He wrote:

> Regulations such as this starved the British army with cold and hunger, while ship loads of stores . . . lay till they perished in Baklava Bay.
>
> . . . [O]rders are sent by telegraph. Contracts are thus made with persons a thousand miles away. If we are to trammel every purchase with new conditions of writing, of record, of affidavit, no human brain will be capable of conducting the business of the great supply departments of the Army.
>
> The Quartermaster's department contains many officers who are, in this time of public extremity, taxed to the limit of their energies in providing the means of moving the Army- wagons, horses, mules, forage, tools, tents, clothing, for the thousands who are actually suffering for want of it.
>
> If, in addition to these duties, they are called upon to record in writing every verbal contract; to put it upon a certain piece of printed paper of a certain shape; to go before a magistrate and take every case a certain oath; delay, irresolution, inefficiency, will take the place of promptness and energy; suffering, discontent, and defeat will attend our armies.[33]

Meigs made his point and the bill did not pass. Congress did require that all purchases and contracts for services be advertised and time allowed for bids to be presented, with the contract going to the lowest bidder. They did make provisions for this to be bypassed in emergency cases and for the need to keep campaign planning secret, but this was to be the exception to the rule.[34] The decentralized purchasing system would stay in place until

1864 when Congress passed a law requiring the bureaus to centralize approval of contracts in Washington.[35]

Lincoln had had enough of Cameron by January 1862. In that month he appointed him Minister to Russia and appointed former attorney general and corporate lawyer Edwin M. Stanton as his replacement. The overbearing, detail-oriented, workaholic Stanton told a group of officers a few weeks after his appointment that, "it is my work to furnish the means, the instruments, for prosecuting the war for the Union and putting down the rebellion against it. It is your duty to use those instruments, and mine to see that you do use them."[36] He quickly proved that he meant what he said. By the end of his first month as Secretary of War, Stanton had appointed John Tucker as Assistant Secretary of War to oversee the contracting for all steamers, transports, wagon-trains, and transportation in general and Colonel Daniel C. McCallum as Military Director and Superintendent of Railroads (which nominally fell under the Quartermaster Department). He also issued a decree to finally clear up the contracting mess caused by Cameron's poor management:

> 1st. That no further contracts be made by this department for any article of foreign manufacture that can be produced in the United States.
> 2d. All outstanding orders for the purchase of arms, clothing, or anything else, in foreign countries are hereby revoked.
> 3d. All persons claiming to have a contract, order, or authority of whatsoever nature, from this Department for furnishing arms, clothing, equipment, or anything else to the United States are required within fifteen days of this date to give written notice of such a contract, with a statement in writing of what has been done under it.
> 4th. It is seldom that any necessary can prevent a contract from being reduced to writing, and even when made by telegraph its terms can be speedily written and signed; and every claim founded on any pretended contract, agreement or license now standing, of which notice and a copy is not filed in accordance with this order, shall be deemed fraudulent and void.[37]

Mr. Stanton and the bureau chiefs had finally brought some order to the procurement process.

Another issue the bureaus had to deal with was paying for all the materiel they were receiving. The level of expenditure was far greater than anything the country had experienced before. New and creative ways of funding the war were necessary. Secretary Chase borrowed money using government bonds for collateral that really amounted to forced loans from banks.[38] Thaddeus Stevens, Chairman of the House Ways and Means Committee, pushed through laws that enabled $150 million in federal paper money, or "greenbacks," to be issued (with only the backing of government bonds and not gold reserves) to pay soldiers and then gave Lincoln's government the ability to borrow $900 million to pay its increasing debts.[39] Even with these measures and increased taxes, tariffs, and bonds, the national debt rose from $65,000,000 at the beginning of the war to $2,678,000,000 by the end.[40] Contracting officers still had serious difficulties paying what was owed to the firms they did business with. Most often they issued certificates of indebtedness once the goods were delivered or services were rendered. It could take up to eighteen months for the funds to come available for those certificates to be paid off.[41]

The supply bureaus were organized and did business in the following manner:

Quartermaster Department

This was the most diverse, and in many ways most important, bureau of the War Department. Its duties were outlined in the Army regulations as:

> This department provides the quarters and transportation of the army; storage and transportation of all army supplies; army clothing; camp and garrison equipment; cavalry and artillery horses; fuel; forage; straw; material for bedding; and stationary. The incidental expenses of the army paid through the Quartermaster's Department include per diem to extra-duty men; postage of public service; the

> expenses of courts-martial, of the pursuit and apprehension of deserters, of the burials of officers and soldiers, of hired escorts, of expresses, interpreters, spies, and guides, of veterinary surgeons and medicines for horses, and of supplying posts with water; and generally the proper and authorized expenses for the movements and operations of any army not expressly assigned to any other departments.[42]

The history of the department between the War of 1812 and the Civil War was dominated by Brevet Major General (MG) Thomas Jesup. MG Jesup served as the Quartermaster General from 1818 until his death in 1860. He supported the army through the Seminole and Mexican Wars as well as the garrisons of the western frontier and put in place many of the systems that led to the success of the department in the Civil War.[43] Brigadier General Joseph E. Johnson succeeded Jesup, but he resigned his commission to go with the South after Virginia seceded. He was replaced by a Captain of the Engineers who had made a name for himself as the builder of the Washington Aqueduct and the expansion of the Capitol building, Montgomery C. Meigs. Brigadier General (BG) Meigs wrote his father that while a lieutenant general commands the army and a major general commands a corps, the quartermaster general supplies the means of moving that army and his command extends from the Atlantic to the Pacific, from the Lakes to the Gulf and so was "second place not in military rank but in actual influence over the war."[44] His efforts in creating a functioning bureau staff, regional depots, forward bases, contracting standards, dispersing millions of dollars, and planning the movements of hundreds of thousands of men made an enormous contribution to the war effort. Secretary of State William Seward's estimate of Meigs' impact was "that without the services of this eminent soldier the national cause must have been lost or deeply imperiled." He would serve throughout the war and retire in 1882.[45]

Many of the commodities needed by the peacetime frontier army were manufactured by the War Department itself. Clothing was made at the Schuykill Arsenal in Philadelphia. Cloth was purchased from textile mills, cut into patterns at the arsenal and sent to tailors and seamstresses to be hand sewn together.[46] (A similar system was in place for making leather shoes.)[47] This system worked for the 16,000-man peacetime army, but could not keep up with the new demand. The clothing depots in Philadelphia, New York, and Cincinnati were the principal centers for clothing procurement.[48] This need for clothing never ceased since the clothing had to be replaced during active campaigning. The standard annual clothing issue for United States soldiers was two caps, one hat, two dress coats, three pairs of trousers, three flannel shirts, three pairs of flannel drawers, four pairs of stockings, and four pairs of bootees with a value totaling $42.[49] Canvas duck was the material used for tentage and was in short supply during the war. To help alleviate this problem, the use of the 20-man Sibley tents was discontinued and each man was issued a shelter half. Two halves buttoned together made a small tent popularly called the "dog" or "pup" tent; a similar design is still in use today.[50] (General William S. Rosecrans issued these to his Army of the Cumberland in the winter of 1863 and they would be used throughout the Tullahoma and Chickamauga campaigns.)[51] In the course of the war, the Quartermaster Department purchased 2,985,000 jackets and 3,500,000 yards of cloth, 7,700,000 trousers, 5,900,000 woolen blankets, and 10,860,000 pairs of shoes.[52] The cost of procuring even a part of this requirement and transporting it to the soldiers ran in the millions each year.

The Quartermaster Department was also responsible for obtaining the draft animals and riding horses for the army. With horses and mules being the primary power for land transport, an adequate supply of them was critical to the mobility of Civil War armies. Early in the war, there was no centralized procurement of animals, the regional depots were responsible for contracting with suppliers for deliver of the animals. This led to a great many useless, unhealthy animals being supplied to the army.[53] The haphazard transportation of the animals and poor care of them in the field also led to a great many animals breaking down under the strain. The quartermaster in Nashville reported in March 1863 that 3,872 horses and 799 mules arrived in Nashville for Rosecrans' army, but 3,391 horses and 735 mules were returned to Louisville. By May, Rosecrans had received 18,000 horses, but he had returned 9,000 to Louisville with another 6,000 more classified as unserviceable still with his army.[54] This critical problem was partially solved in July 1863 with the creation of the Cavalry Bureau, though the reform would not show positive effects until January 1864 with the appointment of Brigadier General James H. Wilson as Bureau Chief. The new bureau was empowered to purchase serviceable horses for the cavalry and to collect, train, care, and distribute them to the units; to provide all the accoutrements needed; and to rehabilitate sick or injured horses. Wilson made his mark in this field when he arrested several businessmen for not fulfilling their contracts with the government during wartime. Six of them were convicted by a court-martial and spent the remainder of the war in the Old Capitol Prison in Washington.[55] The issues that the Quartermaster Department had in keeping Rosecrans Cavalry Corps supplied with mounts was a contributing factor to the creation of this new bureau.

The sheer numbers of animals needed to keep the armies moving were staggering. For the fiscal year 1863, which ran from 1 July 1862 to 30 June 1863, the Quartermaster Department purchased 174,832 horses and 86,254 mules, at an average cost of $120 per animal. A total of 57,576 horses and 17,170 mules were condemned, sold, worn out, captured, or destroyed in the same year.[56] This critical area of supply was a never-ending demand throughout the war.

Forage for the horses and for the mules was a large and bulky commodity that was difficult to store and transport. Each horse needed 14 pounds of hay and 12 pounds of grain (oats, corn, or barley) each day. Mules needed 14 pounds of hay and 9 pounds of grain per day.[57] As armies moved into new territory, they could gather a great deal of the forage they needed from the local area. As weeks passed by, more and more forage had to be shipped in utilizing river, rail and wagon transports. This was a constant burden on the Department of the Cumberland quartermasters who shipped forage to middle Tennessee mainly from St Louis, Missouri, a long journey involving multiple unloadings and repackings on riverboats, barges, and railcars.[58] When the Union forces entered Nashville in February 1862, the quartermasters found 550,000 pounds of corn, 500,000 pounds of oats, and 600,000 pounds of hay in the city that was abandoned by the retreating Confederates. This immense stockpile only met the needs of the Army of the Ohio for a few days. By the end of March 1862, 11 million pounds of forage had arrived in the Nashville depot.[59] The Quartermaster Department had to furnish 2.5 million bushels of grain and 50,000 tons of hay to the US Army each month.[60] The purchasing, storing, and inventorying of this commodity was a primary activity of the Quartermaster Department and had an immense impact on the department's transportation capabilities:

> More often than not transportation is at the very heart of logistical efforts. Occasions when industrial capacity, or the procurement program, or the availability of raw materials determines the extent of the total logistical effort probably are less common than those when transportation is the limiting factor. In

> the Civil War . . . the logistical limitations in the South were nowhere more evident than in the transportation system.[61]

Within the transportation responsibilities of the Quartermaster Department were three distinctly different modes of transport--water (coastal and rivers), railroads, and wagons. Often, commodities would travel on all three on their journey from manufacturer to soldier. Since the largest armies and the most active departments were inland from the coast, rivers were the critical means of resupplying by water. The men and supplies moved by water were not shipped on US naval vessels but on transportation vessels chartered (a more costly method) or contracted from civilian firms. Assistant Secretary of War John Tucker was made the general agent of transportation for the first eighteen months of the war. Tucker and his agents took much of the power from the quartermasters in regard to contracting for vessels (their role by regulation); the quartermasters were little more than clerks processing the agents' paperwork. The quartermasters were still responsible for getting the supplies to the ships and loaded on board (this situation changed back to the quartermasters contracting for the vessels after Tucker resigned in 1862).[62] The water transport system was more problematic in that while the government could make contracts with a railroad company to move freight on its lines, it had to contract with numerous ships captains and owners for every individual vessel used. It was a time-consuming and disjointed process with lots of opportunity for fraud.[63]

In the Western Theater, the major rivers of the region became natural avenues of invasion because they were the easiest means of transporting large numbers of men and quantities of materiel into the enemy's territory. The Ohio, Mississippi, Tennessee, and Cumberland Rivers were important to the logistics of invading armies because of the large amount of cargo a river steamer or barge could carry in a single trip. An average Ohio River steamer held 500 tons (though they ranged from 250-to-1,700-ton capacities). This was enough food and forage to support 70,000 men and 20,000 animals for a day.[64] In comparison, a wagon could hold 2,000 to 2,500 pounds and a railcar 10 tons.[65]

Colonel (COL) Lewis B. Parsons, Chief Quartermaster of River and Rail Transport for the Western Theater who worked out of St. Louis, negotiated the following prices for shipping men and supplies on the western rivers in 1862--½ cent per mile for soldiers with deck accommodations, 1 cent per mile for an officer with a cabin, horses and mules were 1 cent per mile, wagons 1 ¼ cents per mile, and freight 7 cents for each 100 pounds for each 100 miles. Rates did run 25 percent higher on the Ohio and Cumberland Rivers than on the Mississippi. This was because on the Ohio and Cumberland the chartering, or leasing, method of obtaining vessels was initiated early in the war and did not get replaced with COL Parsons' system until 1863. This meant ship owners were paid a set amount of money for their services no matter how much they hauled. The contract system, being a payment system based on weight or items hauled per mile, was a greater incentive for efficient transportation practices. It took 123 steamers to supply MG Rosecrans' army in the winter of 1862-1863 under the charter system. When contracting was adopted, it enabled MG Grant and MG Sherman's armies to be supplied utilizing just 66 vessels in the winter of 1863-1864.[66]

The Chief Quartermaster of Western River Transportation at St. Louis reported that in 1863 193,023 troops moved by rail and 135,909 moved by water in his area of responsibility. All categories of supply moved by rail in this same region for the same time period totaled 153,102,100 pounds while 337,912,363 pounds were shipped by water. While a freight train could move from St. Louis to Cincinnati in 30 hours, it took 70 hours for a steamer to make the same trip. However, in sheer tonnage moved, the river transports could move 500 tons between those cities much faster than freight trains could, shuttling back and forth.[67] The issue with the Tennessee and Cumberland Rivers was that they were only navigable in certain times of the year and they had shoals that could not be crossed at certain points along their courses. The Muscle Shoals in Northern Alabama blocked navigation on the Tennessee River going from the Ohio River to Chattanooga, Tennessee, during the low water levels that occurred each summer, and Harpeth Shoals near Clarksville, Tennessee, blocked traffic on the Cumberland River going from the Ohio River to Nashville, Tennessee.[68] The river transports were also susceptible to attacks from the riverbanks and therefore would often travel only in convoys with gunboat escorts.[69] The quartermasters were powerless to hurry this along.

The waterborne transportation of goods was critical to the success of the Union armies. Vast amounts were moved by water that could never have been moved by rail or wagon. For fiscal year 1863 (1 July 1862 to 30 June 1863), the Quartermaster Department transported by water 4,478,143 barrels and kegs of subsistence stores, 102,914 cattle, 386,756 barrels and kegs of ordnance stores, 1,093 cannon, 753,569 barrels and kegs of quartermaster stores, 109,009 animals, 88,438 tons of forage and fuel, and 567,397 men. They employed 32 ships, 42 brigs, 554 schooners, 4 sloops, 72 propeller ships, 88 steam tugs, 12 ferry boats, 13 tow boats, 695 barges, and 1,222 steamers. For all this the department paid $9,476,681 for river transportation and $4,798,385 for ocean.[70] Water transportation made such a large contribution to the war effort that it "could be said that the railroads remained complementary to the older form of transportation."[71] A foreign military observer of the war, the Count of Paris, had this to say about the value of the western rivers, "We shall always find, therefore, that whenever the Federals were supported by a river their progress was certain and their conquests decisive; whilst the success they obtained by following a single line of railways were always precarious, new dangers springing up in their rear in proportion as they advanced."[72]

Railroads played a significant role in warfare for the first time in the Civil War. "The construction of railroads has introduced a new and very important element into war," wrote MG McClellan to President early in the war.[73] The year 1829 saw the first steam locomotive run in the United States, and by the 1840s, railroad companies were being chartered by state legislatures all over the country.[74] By 1860, 20,000 miles of track had been laid in the Northern states while 9,000 existed in the Southern states. Most of the track in the Southern states ran north-south, linking the Ohio River and the Gulf with the interior. The lines that were built rarely ran the length of a state but merely ran between cities with little ability to link with adjacent rail lines due to varying rail gauges. It was a network of short lines, each built and run by separate companies and requiring frequent loading and unloading of passengers and materiel during transit.[75] The junctions of rail lines at cities like Corinth, Mississippi; Nashville, Tennessee; Chattanooga, Tennessee; Atlanta, Georgia; and Petersburg, Virginia, made those cities prominent military objectives throughout the war; and the rail lines themselves became corridors for invasion, just like rivers had traditionally been.

Rail lines naturally were built to fill a gap in the geography where waterways did not flow. As such, they opened up vast areas of the country for large armies to operate in and through. In the past, when armies moved away from waterways where they could be easily resupplied, they were forced to rely on the muscle power of draft animals pulling wagons to move their materiel. As armies grew larger, more draft animals were needed to haul supplies. There was a diminishing return when increasing the number of draft animals since the forage for those animals also had to be hauled. Food for animals often constituted half of an army's supply requirements. This logistical burden meant that armies relying on draft animals for transport could at best carry ten days of supply with them.[76] It greatly limited the range and independence of field armies.

There were several advantages of using trains instead of animals for transport. First, locomotives could haul more supplies a farther distance on a given amount of fuel than a horse or mule:

> A team of six mules drawing a wagon carrying 1.5 tons of supplies could travel approximately 333 miles on one ton of food. Multiplying 1.5 tons by 333 miles yields 50 ton-miles of transport capacity generated by that ton of mule forage. In contrast, a Civil War-era freight locomotive could travel only thirty-five miles or so on a ton of fuel, but its payload could be as high as 150 tons, yielding 5,250 ton-miles per ton of fuel consumed.[77]

Second, trains traveled five times faster than mule-drawn wagons with the supplies and soldiers hauled on the lines arriving at their destination in much better condition. Third, unlike with horses and mules, locomotives do not consume any fuel when not in use. Fourth, unlike horses and mules, locomotive manufacturing could be increased to meet transportation demands.[78] Railroads were not merely a nice addition to the logistical support provided in the war, they were an absolute necessity to the Union cause. Without them, the massive armies that subdued the South could not have maneuvered around the country and completed their missions. MG William T. Sherman said this about the railroad line that ran from Louisville, KY to Atlanta, GA during his 1864 Atlanta Campaign:

> That single stem of railroad, four hundred and seventy-three miles long, supplied an army of one hundred thousand men and thirty-five thousand animals for a period of one hundred and ninety-six days, viz., May 1 to November 1, 1864. To have delivered regularly that amount of food and forage by ordinary wagons would have required thirty-six thousand eight hundred wagons of six mules each, allowing each wagon to have hauled two tons twenty miles each day, a simple impossibility in roads such as then existed in that region of the country. Therefore, I reiterate that the Atlanta Campaign was an impossibility without these railroads.[79]

An adequate rail line had numerous sidings to allow the passage of trains around each other, platforms and warehouses at stations for unloading and storing supplies, and a "wye" (a three-point-triangle of track that allowed trains to turn and reverse course), and a telegraph to coordinate train movements. The newly constructed railroads of the South rarely had these assets available in an adequate number. Also, the tracks invading armies found were rarely in proper working order due to deterioration from overuse, poor maintenance, lack of materiel, and wartime destruction. Many of the rails were not even made of iron, but were wood with a "U" shaped piece of iron fitted over them.[80] The Union forces were forced to expend great quantities of manpower and money to repair and keep in working order the railroads of the South.

The Federal government did not operate a single mile of rail at the beginning of the war but they would find it militarily necessary to be managing 2,000 miles by war's end.[81] The War Department realized early in the war that coordinating the use of railroads would be vital to the war effort. Secretary of War Simon Cameron appointed the experienced Thomas Scott, who was vice-president of the Pennsylvania Railroad, to coordinate the shipment of supplies and men by rail into Washington. His authority was later broadened when he was put in charge of all railroads and telegraph lines in the country and appointed an Assistant Secretary of War.[82] In January 1862, Congress authorized the president to seize control of railroads for military use in emergencies. A new bureau within the Quartermaster Department was created called the US Military Rail Roads (USMRR) to oversee this management with Colonel, later Brigadier General, Daniel McCallum as director and superintendent. In normal practice, the War Department cooperated with rail companies to meet their logistical needs, though the threat of being taken over by the government was a strong motivator to ensure that cooperation. The USMRR was generally only concerned with the maintenance and running of railroads in the occupied areas of the South where railroad corporations were not functioning.[83] While BG McCallum organized the railroads, it was the quartermasters that supplied the materiel needed for rebuilding and operating the lines, to include locomotives and rolling stock.[84]

Starting in 1862, the USMRR employed civilian construction crews in Virginia under BG Herman Haupt, who was Chief of Construction and Transportation in that region.[85] This was not the case until 1864 in the Western Theater. Until then, generals controlled the railroads that fell within their areas of responsibility. In MG William S. Rosecrans' Department of the Cumberland had COL J. B Anderson, formerly Superintendent of the Louisville and Nashville Railroad, as its Director of Railroads (until his dismissal just prior to Chickamauga when he was replaced by Colonel William P. Innes).[86] The construction, refurbishing, and maintenance of the railroads in that department was done by the railroad corporations, the 1st Michigan Engineers and Mechanics Regiment (the sole engineering unit in the department) and a Pioneer Brigade of engineers and laborers organized by MG Rosecrans. The quartermasters were in a partnership with the director of railroads, engineers, USMRR, and the civilian railroad corporations in the shipment of men and materiel on the rail lines in the Department of the Cumberland.

The government had to pay for the use of these civilian rail lines, like any other customer. In 1861, the schedule of rates agreed to by Mr. Scott allowed unnecessarily high rates to be charged, 1/3 more than to private parties. Secretary of War Edwin Stanton called a meeting of railroad managers in early 1862 that divided supplies being shipped into four categories:

> The first class of supplies was drums, haversacks, camp kettles, furniture, clothing, powder in barrels or secure packages. Second class was small arms, wagons, mounted guns and caissons, medicines, coffee, tea, harness, horses, cattle and mules. Third class was ammunition, Sibley stoves, and tools. Fourth class was unmounted artillery, cannon balls and shells, horseshoes, lumber, nuts, bolts, washers, nails, spikes, wire, rope, rations and forage. Rates for short hauls varied from five cents per ton-mile for first class supplies to four cents per ton-mile for fourth class supplies; for longer hauls they ranged from three cents per ton-mile for first class to one and three-fourths cents per ton-mile for fourth class. The regulations stipulated that the military tariff should be ten percent below the printed freight tariffs of the various companies in force at the time.[87]

For fiscal year 1863 (1 July 1862-30 June 1863), the Quartermaster Department transported by rail 784,833 barrels and kegs and 17,654 cattle in subsistence stores; 354,659 barrels and kegs and 883 guns and others in ordnance stores; 430,666 barrels and packages, 126,584 animals, 39,354 tons of forage, fuel and other quartermaster stores; and 1,264,602 troops; this cost a total of $8,030,003.[88] This expense enabled the Union war machine to drive deep into the interior of the Confederacy.

Quartermaster General Meigs stated that a "railroad is an engine of war more powerful than a battery of artillery," and railroads "supplied [the] armies, and enabled them to move and accomplish in weeks what without them would have required years, or would have been impossible."[89] Railroads were what enabled the enormous Union armies to get into the Confederate interior and win the war.

Once the supplies reached the riverbank or the railroad terminal, they had to be moved to the troops for distribution or carried along on a campaign. This was done through the use of wagons pulled by teams of six mules. A wagon and team was capable of hauling 4,000 pounds on good roads under ideal weather conditions. Since this was rarely the case when armies were moving across country, the usual wagonload was around 2,400 pounds, which included forage for the team. The standard army wagon cost $125 and mules (which were preferred to horses because of their better endurance and smaller forage requirement) cost $125 each. The total cost for a wagon was $900 with an additional $3 a day cost for maintenance and forage.[90]

With each wagon and team occupying 12 yards of road space, a column of 800 wagons would stretch for 6 to 8 miles on the march. There was no regulation standardizing the number of wagons in general supply trains since each campaign dictated its own requirements, so each army commander issued his own directives in this regard. An obvious rule was the fewer the wagons being hauled, the faster the army could move. MG Henry Halleck observed, "Once accustomed to a certain amount of transport, an army is unwilling to do without the luxuries which it supplies in the field." Because of this, commanders were forever battling to keep down the size of their wagon trains. Napoleon's ideal ratio of wagons to men was 12.5 per 1,000. This was rarely achieved by Union armies. LTG Grant allowed 19 per thousand, MG McClellan had 26 per thousand,

and MG Banks had 91 per thousand. (The problems with too much baggage affected mobility in many campaigns to include Tullahoma and Chickamauga.)[91]

The wagon trains consisted of headquarters, regimental, and the general supply trains. While the general supply trains were unlimited, the headquarters and regimental trains were limited in 1862. These baggage trains were set at four wagons for a corps headquarters, three for the headquarters of a division or brigade, six for a regiment, and three for a battery.[92] A typical regiment employed its wagons as follows: one wagon for medical stores, one wagon for tents and baggage of field and staff officers, one wagon for baggage of line officers, one wagon for kettles and pans for ten companies, one wagon for medical supplies, two wagons for two days' rations for men, and five days' rations for animals.[93] As an example of the number of wagons involved in moving an army, in 1864, LTG Grant set the following allowance for general supply wagons for the armies operating against Richmond: 7 per 1,000 men for subsistence and forage, 50 per cavalry division for forage exclusively, 4 wagons for each battery of artillery for subsistence and forage, 3 wagons per brigade for medical supplies, and 3 subsistence and forage wagons per corps headquarters with 2 per division and 1 per brigade.[94]

BG Rufus Ingalls, Chief Quartermaster for the Army of the Potomac, wrote this in regard to his operating principles for his trains:

> In a forward movement our trains are never in the way of the troops; on the contrary each corps has its train which follows it on the march, and which forms its indispensable, movable magazine of supplies. Wagon trains should never be permitted to approach within range of the battlefields. They should be parked in safe and convenient places out of risk, and well guarded. Troops should go forward into battle lightly loaded, and without wagons except for extra ammunition. If they are successful, the trains can be brought up very quickly; if defeated, they will find an unobstructed road, and will get back to their wagons soon enough.

BG Ingalls also started the practice of labeling the wagons with their respective corps badges after they were adopted in 1863. He also required that the contents of the wagons be marked on the outside of the wagon. These simple innovations greatly aided in tracking supplies on the move. [95]

The amount of forage needed by draft animals, 26 pounds for horses and 23 for mules each day, limited the distance that wagons could operate away from the supply depots. MG Sherman felt that an army could not operate more than 100 miles from its supply base because after that distance, the teams would consume all the contents of the wagons they were hauling. The Count of Paris wrote this excellent description of American supply issues in the Civil War:

> The American wagon, drawn by six mules, carries a load of 2,000 pounds, sufficient, therefore, to supply 500 men, provided they can make the trip daily, going and returning, between the army and its depots. If the distance to be traveled is such as to require a whole days march, one day being lost in returning empty, it will only be able to supply 500 men every other day, or 250 daily. To go a distance of two days march from its base of operations is a very small matter for an army that is maneuvering in front of the enemy, and yet, according to this computation, it will require four wagons to supply 500 men with provisions, or eight for 1,000, and consequently 800 for 100,000. If this army of 100,000 men has 16,000 cavalry and artillery horses, a small number comparatively speaking, 200 more wagons will be required to carry their daily forage, and therefore, 800 to transport it to a distance of two days march. These 1,600 wagons are, in their turn, drawn by 9,600 mules, which, also consuming twenty-five pounds during each of the three days out of four they are away from the depot, require 360 wagons more to carry their forage; these 360 wagons are drawn by 2,400 animals, and in order to transport the food required by the latter, 92 additional wagons are necessary. Adding twenty wagons more for general purposes, we shall find that 2,000 wagons, drawn by 12,000 animals, are strictly necessary to victual an army of 100,000 men and 16,000 horses at only two days march from its base of operations. In the same proportion, if this army finds itself separated from its base of operations by three days march, 3,760 wagons, drawn by 22,000 animals, will be found indispensable for that service.[96]

The connection between the resupply depots (located at rivers and railheads) can be clearly understood by this description. It was a staggering proposition to keep a Civil War army supplied with just food and forage, let alone ammunition, clothing, etc, once it left the vicinity of its forward depots. If a region of the country could not be foraged from and most everything had to be carried in wagons with the army moving and fighting in that region (like the Army of the Cumberland in August and September 1863), the commander's difficulties were greatly multiplied.

To enable its armies to operate in the field, the Quartermaster Department supplied the following at the end of fiscal year 1863: 197,457 horses, 119,068 mules, 17,796 army wagons, 4,166 ambulances, 1,263 light wagons and 154,357 wheel and lead harnesses.[97] The logisticians had tremendous challenges to overcome to allow commanders the freedom to maneuver in campaigns.

The quartermasters were also responsible for hiring and supervising all of the civilian workers needed as clerks, laborers, and teamsters in the supply depots and with the armies.[98] A chief clerk of a depot could earn as much as $100 a month, while a laborer used for loading and unloading supplies would earn $30 a month. This was true for both whites and blacks during the Union occupation of Nashville, TN, which was possible only because of the severe lack of available laborers in the region.[99] Rates varied from place to place, going up when the dangers and discomforts increased.

The quartermasters were responsible for providing warehouses, offices, barracks, hospitals, and houses for the soldiers and civilians in their depots and training areas. They could either rent the structures or build them. Often the first troops in an area were provided materials and had to build their own barracks.[100] In urban areas, such as Washington or Nashville, buildings were rented by force if necessary. Prices could range from $100 a month for a large warehouse to $37.50 a month for a large home. The value of the property was set by the quartermasters so it often was not a fair market price for the area.[101]

In a bureaucracy during a time before typewriters and computers, everything had to be hand written. To bring some semblance of order to the paperwork of the War Department, forms and ledgers were printed for all Army bookkeeping, correspondence, orders, and others. It was the job of the quartermasters to supply it. They also provided blank sheets of paper, envelopes, pens, bottles of black ink, and spools of office tape or ribbon, better known as government "red tape."[102] It was just another of the many varied duties that fell to the invaluable Quartermasters of the Union army.

Commissary Department

The Commissary Department managed a single commodity, food for human consumption. At the time, this was deemed to be so different in its procurement, storage and transport that a separate bureau with its own dedicated officers was responsible to provide it to the field armies, prisoners of war, and loyal families in invaded areas of the South[103]. COL George Gibson had been the Commissary General of Subsistence for 43 years when he died in September 1861. His replacement, BG Joseph P. Taylor was a veteran of 32 years of service. He died in office in June 1864 and was replaced by BG Amos B. Eaton who served until the end of the war.[104] At the start of the war, the department only had 12 officers assigned to it; by 1863 that had been increased to 29, but the department was augmented by 535 volunteer commissary officers. By war's end, the Commissary Department had disbursed $361,786,991.83.[105]

The Commissary Department mirrored the Quartermaster Department in its organization. The department staff was located in Washington with major depots set up in

Boston, New York, Philadelphia, Baltimore, Cincinnati, Louisville, Chicago, and St. Louis to purchase supplies and gather them for shipment.[106] Normally these Commissary Depots were co-located with the Quartermaster Depots since the quartermasters actually organized the transport of subsistence goods (the quartermasters shipped 146,594 tons of foodstuffs by rail and 174,217 tons of foodstuffs by water in 1863).[107] This was also true at the geographical departments and forward depots.

Since subsistence stores were "cash articles," meaning prompt payment was necessary to purchase them, the Commissary Department did have a better record for paying its debts than the quartermasters did.[108] Most food items were purchased using a bid system. The local commissary officer would advertise for a quantity of items, accept bids from suppliers, and chose the lowest bidder to purchase from. This was also true for purchasing flour, though normally this was acquired closer to the armies in the field. Beef was done through contracts. The cattle were shipped to the geographic department depots and driven to the army (and with the army when it moved).[109]

The 1861 Army regulations authorized the following ration per day per soldier. (This was slightly increased in 1862 but returned to this authorization in 1864.)

20 oz. of salt or fresh beef or 12 oz. of pork or bacon
18 oz. of flour or 20 oz. of corn meal
1.6 oz. of rice or .64 oz. of beans or 1.5 oz. of dried potatoes
1.6 oz. of green coffee or .24 oz. of tea
2.4 oz. of sugar
.54 oz. of salt
.32 gill of vinegar

The famous "marching ration" for the Union army was:

1 pound of hard bread (hardtack)
¾ pounds of salt pork or ¼ pounds of fresh meat
1 oz. of coffee
3 oz. of sugar, and salt.

For planning purposes, the weight of one ration was calculated at 3 pounds.[110]

Rations were signed for down the chain from army, division, and brigade commissary chiefs. The regimental quartermaster, as the sole logistics officer in his unit, would sign for the food with his regimental commissary sergeant taking charge of it. Rations were normally issued four days worth at a time.[111] The cattle driven along with the units would be slaughtered at the brigade level and issued the day before expected consumption.[112] Whenever the troops were in camp for any amount of time, bakeries were set up to provide fresh bread.[113] In garrison, cooking was done at the company level with the soldiers' rations being combined for meals. In the field, it was done individually or in small groups.[114]

Dried vegetables and canned foods were also available in the war, though not a regular part of the ration. The Louisville Depot shipped 110 gallons of canned cabbage, 34,860 cans of tomatoes, 26,856 cans of peaches, 23,112 cans of assorted fruit, 18,192 cans of oysters, 25,440 cans of condensed milk, and 5,820 cans of jelly between 1 January and 1 August 1864.[115] Fresh fruits and vegetables were obtained as close to the troops as possible to lessen spoilage, though these rarely got to soldiers on the march. Soldiers could also supplement their diet through foraging, purchasing food through sutlers and receiving donated goods through civilian sanitary commissions.[116]

The Commissary General reported in 1861 to the Secretary of War, that never before in history had an army been so well supplied. The Union soldier did receive double the ration of a Prussian soldier and 20 percent more than a British soldier.[117] So while the Union soldiers often had a monotonous diet, they rarely went hungry thanks to the Commissary Departments efforts.

Ordnance Department

> "Young man, are you aware that every shot you fire costs the government two dollars and sixty-seven cents?"- Brevet MG Henry Hunt, Chief of Artillery for the Army of the Potomac, to a young battery commander who failed to properly sight his guns between firing them.[118]

The Ordnance Department was responsible for all the arsenals (where arms are manufactured) and armories (where arms are stored) of the US Army and was responsible for furnishing all ordnance required (rifles, pistols, cannon, small arms cartridges, artillery rounds, black powder, artillery fuses, and accoutrements to operate these weapons, like cartridge boxes, percussion caps, cannon sponges, etc). The Chief of Ordnance was headquartered in Washington with major arsenals in Watervliet, New York; St. Louis; Washington; Kennebec, Massachusetts; and Alleghany, Pennsylvania.[119] Ordnance depots were co-located with quartermaster depots because it was the quartermasters who arranged transportation for the ordnance stores until it reached the armies, when the ordnance wagons became the means of transport. (The Quartermaster Department transported 72,776 tons [including 883 cannons] of ordnance stores by rail and 78,088 tons [including 1,093 cannons] by water in fiscal year 1863.)[120]

As the war began in April 1861, COL Henry K. Craig was replaced as Chief of Ordnance by BG James W. Ripley. BG Ripley was replaced in September 1863 by BG George D. Ramsay who in turn was replaced by BG Alexander B. Dyer in September

1864.[121] Like the other logistical bureau's of the War Department, the Ordnance Department had a very small regular army staff and needed hundreds of volunteer officers to execute its duties. Having to appoint "acting" ordnance officers led to a great deal of confusion in the field and was complained about by BG Dyer in his fiscal year 1865 annual report.[122]

When the war began, the lack of weapons available in the United States to arm volunteers became a critical problem. To alleviate the pressure until the government and civilian manufacturing could be increased, the US government sent purchasing agents to Europe to buy weapons. In the first 15 months of the war, 738,000 muskets, rifles, and carbines were purchased there for the Union armies. Many of these were obsolete weapons the European armies were happy to be rid of.[123] While the standard US Army weapon was the .58 Springfield muzzle-loading rifle musket, the number of foreign weapons (British, French, Belgian, Austrian and Prussian) in the inventory numbered approximately 550,000 compared to the 802,000 Springfields used in the war. There were also thousands of smoothbore, breech-loading, and repeating rifles in use in the armies. All of these different caliber and types of weapons led to great difficulties providing ammunition and repair parts to the soldiers in the field.[124]

Private industry produced all of the artillery (the carriages and caissons were made at the arsenals), all the gunpowder, and a large portion of the small arms used by the North in the war. Of the 802,000 Springfields manufactured in the war, 670,600 came from private firms. The cost of a Springfield made in a government arsenal was $10, in a civilian factory $20.[125]

The Ordnance Department has come down through history as being anti-innovation in regards to repeating rifles. BG Ripley in particular has been ridiculed for not wanting to provide repeating rifles to the armies. It must be understood, however, that the Ordnance Department had trouble arming the forces with even obsolete firearms, let alone a new rifle without a major manufacturing plant. Also, the Ordnance Department was struggling to try and standardize weapons within regiments and brigades, the last thing it felt it needed was yet another type weapon and caliber of ammunition to supply. In the end, repeating rifles made it into the army (200,000 Spencers alone) and had a significant impact on several campaigns starting in 1863.[126]

The Ordnance Department's single biggest contractor in the war was the West Point Iron and Cannon Foundry which was awarded 2,332 separate contracts for a total of $4,733,059. Colt's Patent Fire Arms Company was awarded 267 contracts for a total of $4,687,031. In Fiscal Year 1863, the Ordnance Department purchased the following items at a cost of $45,000,000:

1,126 cannon of different calibers
1,099,622 cannon balls and shells
1,082,841 small arms for foot soldiers
282,389 small arms for mounted troops
901,667 sets of infantry accoutrements
18,009 sets of cavalry accoutrements
1,435, 046 rounds of artillery ammunition
259,022,216 rounds of ammunition for small arms
347,276,400 percussion caps.[127]

The size of the unit ordnance trains was not set by regulation but by the local army commanders, just like the quartermasters' trains, depending on the need for each campaign. Ammunition for the muzzle loading rifles came in a hand-rolled paper cartridge that contained the lead minié ball and a powder charge. These were wrapped in paper and tied with string in bundles of 10 and 1,000 rounds were packed together in a wood crate marked with the type of cartridge and the date and place of manufacture. Percussion caps for these rounds normally came packed with the rounds. Each crate weighed 98 pounds. Normally, an Army supply wagon could haul a maximum of 2,500 pounds. This meant that one wagon could haul up to 25 crates containing 25,000 rounds of ammunition.[128] Soldiers carried 40 rounds in the cartridge boxes and 20 rounds in their knapsacks on the march. The brigade and division trains tried to carry the equivalent of another 40 rounds per man and the corps trains another 100 per man.[129]

The multiple types of field artillery pieces each carried a different amount of ammunition with them. Each smoothbore artillery round came in its own pre-sized cloth cartridge with a measured amount of black powder and the rifled guns rounds had detached pre-sized powder charges. The standard ammunition chest for a 12-pounder cannon held 32 rounds; that for a 3-inch ordnance rifle and the 10-pounder Parrott held 50. Each cannon was accompanied by two limbers and a caisson. The limber had one ammunition chest mounted on it and the caisson had two chests. So with four chests per gun, 128 rounds traveled with a 12-pounder, and 200 rounds with a 3-inch ordnance or 10-pounder Parrott. The ordnance trains tried to carry an amount equal to that carried with each gun. There would also be a variety of different types of ammunition carried: solid shot, shell, spherical case, and canister.[130]

Like all the logisticians in the Civil war, the Ordnance Department had enormous challenges to overcome. Through its efforts, the union armies were capably armed and able to fight and win the war.

Medical Department

The Medical Department of the US Army had 27 of its 114 regular army surgeons resign when the South seceded. While the regular officers were the core of the department's leaders, thousands of volunteer and civilian doctors, nurses, and stewards played a large role in completing the department's mission.[131]

This department was headed by the Surgeon General. This position was held by COL Thomas Lawson for 25 years prior to his death of apoplexy in May 1861. He was succeeded for 11 months by COL Clement A. Finley, a man with 40 years experience in the Army but with few skills that would enable him to organize the department in its mammoth task of building an infrastructure from the small number of peacetime surgeons. Because of this he was replaced in April 1862 by the competent but proud BG William A. Hammond. Hammond quickly found himself at odds with equally prideful Secretary of War Stanton. Secretary Stanton used his power to have BG Hammond court-martialed for a minor charge stemming from irregular contracts and dismissed from the service in Aug 1864. He was replaced by BG Joseph K. Barnes who served through the remainder of the war.[132]

Medicine in the United States in the Civil War era was not the profession that we have today. In some areas of the country, only 20 percent of practicing physicians had graduated from a medical school. Even a graduate of one of the 40 medical schools in the country would have only attended a series of anatomy, biology, and chemistry lectures for a school year, and then attended the same ones again the next year. They also would have done some sort of "apprenticeship" under an experienced physician. Since few states had any licensing laws, the person who had passed "the majority" of their tests in school and graduated could be called "doctor."[133] Most of the practicing physicians in the country did not even have this much training. Because of this and the inability of the states and the federal government to comply with mandatory tests for physicians being appointed surgeon or assistant surgeon, a lot of incompetent men were treating the sick and wounded during the early years of the war.

In May 1861, Congress authorized a surgeon and an assistant surgeon for each regiment. Initially, these officers and their tents were the only hospitals outside the small post hospitals on older posts. The General Hospitals had to be created to handle the soldiers that would have lengthy convalescence. These were fixed facilities, either in already existing buildings converted into hospitals (since few civilian hospitals of any size existed) or newly constructed pavilion style hospital with wards connected by covered walks.[134] These facilities were commanded by a uniformed physician, but they were staffed by a mix of people. Uniformed physicians served as ward physicians, as did civilian contract physicians. Hospital stewards were enlisted men who acted as wound dressers, apothecaries, and nurses.[135] Both male and female nurses were employed. While there were only a few crude nursing schools in the country, lessons learned from the British in the Crimean War in the 1850s taught these nurses that cleanliness of the wards and patients, as well as good nutrition, kept disease and infection to a minimum and more patients recovered.[136] (Sadly, lack of sanitation in camps and hospitals led to more deaths from dysentery, typhoid, malaria, and infections than bullets on the battlefield.)[137] If not hired as female nurses by Ms. Dorothea Dix, the "Superintendent of Female Nurses,"[138] nurses were often members of many charity commissions, such as the US Sanitary Commission, that provided doctors and nurses, fresh food, medical supplies, and religious services throughout the war. These organizations even chartered, renovated, and staffed river steamers and railroad cars to transport the sick and wounded from the camps and battlefields of the South to the General Hospitals in Northern cities.[139]

In the Western Theater, the principal general hospitals were in Memphis and Nashville and along the Ohio River. The hospital in Jeffersonville, Indiana, had a bed capacity of 2,600 and cost $250,000 when it was built in the winter of 1863-1864. A hospital of 1,000 beds had upwards of 200 staff members to include 20 stewards, 40 to 100 nurses, cooks, bakers, launderers, carpenters, and others.[140] General Hospitals treated 1,057,423 cases during the war and had a mortality rate of 8 percent.[141]

The treatment of wounded on the battlefield started out a shambles. Lack of qualified surgeons, poor and little medical equipment and supplies, no vehicles dedicated to evacuation, and lack of staff all contributed. Surgeon General Hammond worked for reforms by restricting entry to only qualified surgeons and improving supplies and equipment. Tests were given to all physicians in the service and seeking commissions and slowly the quality of the doctors improved. Medical purveyors (physicians detailed to purchase medical supplies and equipment for the field and garrison medical staffs) were given wider authority, though much of the non-medical supplies they required still had to be obtained from Quartermaster and Commissary officers. The principle medical supply depot was in New York, but every geographic department had their own.[142]

With these reforms taking place at the top levels, the medical directors for the different armies were able to make their own reforms on the battlefield. The most famous medical director of the war was Dr. Jonathan Letterman, Medical Director for the Army of the Potomac in 1862-1863. He instituted three main reforms that revolutionized battlefield casualty evacuation and treatment. First, he convinced MG McClellan to assign all ambulances to the Medical Department instead of with the quartermasters. This stopped them from being used to haul supplies and not be available for patients. He also arranged for permanent details of men to act as stretcher bearers to load patients onto the ambulances at the regimental collection points for transport back to the field hospitals. (There were two types of ambulances, a light, two-wheeled version and a heavier, four wheeled one designed by MG Rosecrans. Both had springs and litter stands built into them.) Second, Dr. Letterman introduced a standard medical supply wagon in each regiment with the same supplies in each. This standardization helped greatly for resupply. Third, he created brigade and division hospitals to consolidate doctors from the various regiments to perform needed surgeries during a battle. The doctors were assigned to their duties on skill, not on rank. These basic reforms greatly improved the medical care in the Army of the Potomac but, as with so many things in the war, local army commanders were the ones who decided most of these standards. It would take until the last year of the war for them to be adopted throughout the army.[143]

The following is a description of battlefield medicine prepared by Surgeon General Barnes after the war:

> After the organization . . . was perfected, the medical service in the field was based upon an independent hospital and ambulance establishment for each division of three brigades. . . . The division ambulance train was commanded by a First Lieutenant of the line, assisted by a Second Lieutenant for each brigade. The enlisted men detailed for ambulance duty were a sergeant for each regiment, three privates for each ambulance, and one private for each wagon. The ambulance train consisted of from one to three ambulances for each regiment, squadron, or battery, a medical wagon for each brigade, and two or more supply wagons. The hospital and ambulance train were under the control of the Surgeon-in-Chief. The division hospitals were usually located just outside of the range of

artillery fire. Sometimes three or more division's hospitals were consolidated under the orders of a Corps Medical Director.[144]

Some statistics on the medical department during the war are: surgeons performed 29,980 amputations (most often due to the soft lead bullets splintering bones on impact) with 7,459 proving fatal,[145] 204 General Hospitals were opened[146] (including 14 in Nashville, TN[147]), 50,000 stretcher were issued to field units,[148] and for the fiscal year 1863 the medical department dispersed $11,594,650 to care for the soldiers of the Union army.[149]

Conclusion

The logistical bureaus of the Union army developed into an efficient machine capable of effectively harnessing the power of the North and bringing it to bear on the Southern Confederacy. The efforts of the quartermaster, ordnance, commissary and medical officers, noncommissioned officers, and civilians made the armies in the field possible. They built organizations from the ground up when the war began. With no blueprint or American historical experience to draw from, the leaders of the North created a massive bureaucracy capable of purchasing, transporting, tracking, and disbursing millions of dollars in commodities and services. The logistical system of the North showed the agility and capability of the US government. It was an unprecedented achievement and one deserving of the highest recognition in American military history.

The North's advantages in population, industry, agriculture, finance, and transportation were overwhelming. The Union cause only needed commanders who were willing and able to focus those advantages on the South to obtain victory. President Lincoln's government turned to MG William Rosecrans and his Army of the Cumberland to create victories in Tennessee. While many factors played into the battles MG

Rosecrans fought in 1863, it was logistical considerations that decided when and where these titanic struggles would take place.

---

[1]Charles R. Schrader, *United States Army Logistics, 1775-1992: An Anthology,* vol. 1 (Honolulu, Hawaii: University Press of the Pacific, 2001), 34.

[2]Shelby Foote, *The Civil War: A Narrative- Fort Sumter to Perryville* (New York, New York: Vintage Books, 1986), 60.

[3]Ibid., 60; and Bruce Catton, *The Coming Fury* (New York, New York: Washington Square Press, 1967), 475.

[4]James M. McPherson, *Battle Cry of Freedom: The Civil War Era* (New York, New York: Oxford University Press, 1988), 95.

[5]Ibid., 100-101.

[6]Richard J. Hathaway, *Michigan: Visions of Our Past* (East Lansing, Michigan: Michigan State University Press, 1989), 104.

[7]Christopher R. Gabel, *Railroad Generalship: Foundations of Civil War Strategy* (Fort Leavenworth, Kansas: Combat Studies Institute, 1997), 22.

[8]McPherson, 92.

[9]Ibid., 92.

[10]Foote, 59.

[11]Schrader, 194.

[12]James A. Huston, *The Sinews of War: Army Logistics, 1775-1953* (Washington, DC: Office of the Chief of Military History, 1966), 102-103.

[13]Ibid., 112-114.

[14] bid., 125.

[15]William J. Cooper, *Jefferson Davis, American* (New York, New York: Alfred A. Knopf, 2000), 245-247.

[16]John S. D. Eisenhower, *Agent of Destiny: The Life and Times of General Winfield Scott* (New York, New York: The Free Press, 1997), 209.

[17]Cooper, 246.

[18]Schrader, 194.

[19]Huston, 175, 183.

[20]David W. Miller, *Second Only to Grant: Quartermaster General Montgomery C. Meigs* (Shippensburg, Pennsylvania: White Mane Books, 2000), 122.

[21]Huston, 166-167.

[22]Ibid., 167.

[23]Ibid., 171-172.

[24]Lenette S. Taylor, *The Supply for Tomorrow Must Not Fail: Civil War of Captain Simon Perkins Jr., a Union Quartermaster* (Kent, Ohio: The Kent State University Press, 2004.), 1-2.

[25]Huston, 174.

[26]Taylor, 12-13.

[27]Miller, 121. Schrader, 197.

[28]Schrader, 198.

[29]Huston, 174-175.

[30]Fletcher Pratt, *Stanton: Lincoln's Secretary of War* (Westport, Connecticut: Greenwood Press, 1953), 152.

[31]Huston, 161.

[32]Ibid.,

[33]Miller, 116.

[34]Erna Risch, *Quartermaster Support of the Army: A History of the Corps, 1775-1939* (Washington, DC: Quartermaster Historian's Office, 1962), 342.

[35]Schrader, 203.

[36]Pratt, 145.

[37]Ibid., 149-150.

[38]Huston, 183.

[39]Hans L. Trefousse, *Thaddeus Stevens: Nineteenth-Century Egalitarian* (Mechanicsburg, Pennsylvania: Stackpole Books, 2001), 131.

[40]Miller, 119.

[41]Taylor, 96.

[42]Ibid., ix-x.

[43]Biographical Sketch of Thomas S. Jesup, Quartermaster Museum Homepage, available from www.qmfound.com, Internet, accessed 10 December 2004.

[44]Miller, 96.

[45]Biographical Sketch of Montgomery C. Meigs, Quartermaster Museum Homepage, available from www.qmfound.com, Internet, accessed on 10 December 2004.

[46]Risch, 348.

[47]Ibid., 360.

[48]Huston, 184.

[49]Schrader, 203.

[50]Schrader, 203-204.

[51]William M. Lamers, *The Edge of Glory: A Biography of General William S. Rosecrans, U.S.A.* (Baton Rouge, Louisiana: Louisiana State University Press, 1999), 253.

[52]Huston, 184.

[53]Schrader, 204.

[54]Taylor, 114.

[55]Edward G. Longacre, *Grant's Cavalryman: The Life and Wars of General James H. Wilson* (Mechanicsburg, Pennsylvania: Stackpole Books, 1972), 96-101.

[56]*Annual Report of the Quartermaster General,* House of Representatives, 38th Congress, Executive Documents (Washington: Government Printing Office, 1863), 64.

[57]Schrader, 205.

[58]Taylor, 25.

[59]Ibid., 24.

[60]Schrader, 205.

[61]Huston, 198.

[62]Risch, 368-372; and Pratt, 148.

[63]Ibid., 406-408.

[64]Schrader, 206; and Huston, 211.

[65]Huston, 208.

[66]Risch, 409-410.

[67]Huston, 211.

[68]Taylor, 23, 49.

[69]Ibid., 24, 151.

[70]Annual Report of the Quartermaster General FY 1863, 65.

[71]Huston, 213.

[72]Ibid., 213.

[73]Schrader, 209.

[74]Christopher R. Gabel, *Railroad Generalship: Foundations of Civil War Strategy* (Fort Leavenworth, Kansas: Combat Studies Institute, Command and General Staff College, 1997), 12.

[75]Schrader, 210.

[76]Gabel, 1.

[77]Ibid., 2-3.

[78]Ibid., 3-4.

[79]Huston, 207.

[80]Gabel, 15-16.

[81]Risch, 395.

[82]Huston, 199.

[83]Ibid., 200-201, Gabel, 13.

[84]Risch, 397, 401.

[85]Huston, 201-204.

[86]Risch, 401.

[87]Huston, 199-200.

[88]Report of the Quartermaster General 1863, 65.

[89]Miller, 113.

[90]Schrader, 206-207.

[91]Ibid., 206-207.

[92]Huston, 216, and Risch, 421.

[93]Risch, 422.

[94]Huston, 216-217.

[95]Schrader, 209.

[96]Huston, 216.

[97]Report of the Quartermaster General 1863, 64.

[98]Huston, 170.

[99]Taylor, 26-27.

[100]Risch, 440-442.

[101]Taylor, 136-137.

[102]Ibid., 54-55.

[103]Kenneth W. Munden and Henry P. Beers, *The Union: A Guide to Federal Archives Relating to the Civil War* (Washington, DC; National Archives and Records Administration, 1986), 313.

[104]Huston, 168; and Schrader, 195.

[105]Munden, 313.

[106]*Annual Report of the Commissary General of Subsistence,* House of Representatives, 38th Congress, Executive Documents (Washington: Government Printing Office, 1864), 46.

[107]Annual Report of the Quartermaster General 1863, 65.

[108]Ibid., 46.

[109]Ibid., 46, Huston, 185.

[110]Schrader, 201.

[111]Huston, 217-218.

[112]Schrader, 202.

[113]Risch, 450.

[114]Huston, 218.

[115]Ibid., 217.

[116]Ibid., 185.

[117]Ibid, 185.

[118]Edward Longacre, *The Man Behind the Guns: A Military Biography of General Henry J. Hunt, Chief of Artillery, Army of the Potomac* (Cambridge, Massachusetts: Da Capo Books, 2003), 11.

[119]Munden, 277.

[120]Annual Report of the Quartermaster General, 1863, 65.

[121]Schrader, 195.

[122]Munden, 278.

[123]Huston, 178-179.

[124]Ibid., 186.

[125]Ibid., 178,186.

[126]Ibid., 188.

[127]*Annual Report of the Chief of Ordnance,* House of Representatives, 38th Congress, Executive Documents (Washington: Government Printing Office, 1863), 102.

[128]John Davis, "The Role of Ordnance Logistics in the Chickamauga Campaign" (thesis, US Army Command and General Staff College: Fort Leavenworth, Kansas, 1995), 22-23.

[129]Schrader, 200.

[130]Ibid., 200.

[131]Mary C. Gillett, *The Medical Department: 1818-1865* (Washington, DC: Center of Military history, 1987), 153.

[132]Gillet, 154; Schrader, 195; and Pratt, 278.

[133]Frank R. Freemon, *Gangrene and Glory: Medical Care During the American Civil War* (Urbana and Chicago, Illinois: University of Illinois Press, 2001), 25; and Paul Starr, *The Social Transformation of American Medicine: The Rise of a Sovereign Profession and the Making of a Vast Industry* (New York, New York: Basic Books, 1982), 63-64, 114.

[134]Gillett, 156.

[135]Ibid., 156.

[136]Ibid., 161.

[137]Ibid., 158.

[138]Huston, 250.

[139]Freemon, 70-71.

[140]Huston, 249.

[141]Ibid., 252.

[142]Gillet, 159.

[143]Freemon, 75.

[144]Huston, 240.

[145]Ibid., 252.

[146]Ibid., 249.

[147]*Annual Report of the Surgeon General,* House of Representatives, 38th Congress, Executive Documents (Washington: Government Printing Office, 1863), 70.

[148]Huston, 241.

[149]Annual Report of the Surgeon General, 67.

CHAPTER 3

LOGISTICS IN THE DEPARTMENT OF THE CUMBERLAND JANUARY TO JUNE 1863

> Since the dawn of history, military strategy has been dominated by the inexorable calculus of logistics- distance, time, transport capacity, and consumption.[1]
>
> Dr. Christopher R. Gabel

On 24 October 1862, the War Department ordered MG Rosecrans to report to Louisville, Kentucky to replace MG Don Carlos Buell.[2] Buell had commanded the Department of the Ohio, but Rosecrans was to command a new department called the Department of the Cumberland. The old Department of the Ohio was split at the Kentucky and Tennessee border. Kentucky stayed as part of the Department of the Ohio under the command of BG Horatio Wright. The area of Tennessee east of the Tennessee River and any area of northern Alabama or Georgia that the army could enter was what encompassed the Department of the Cumberland. The "wings" commanded by MG George Thomas, MG Alexander McCook, and MG Thomas Crittenden, all officially under the designation the XIV Corps, were the field army for the new department. These wings would become Thomas' XIV, McCook's XX, and Crittenden's XXI Corps on 9 January 1863, the same day the army was officially named the Army of the Cumberland.[3] MG Rosecrans' orders from the War Department were to drive the enemy from, and hold, middle and east Tennessee, so as to liberate the Union sympathizers in those regions, and cut the railroad running from Chattanooga to Virginia, thereby severing the shortest route from the eastern to western theaters for the Confederate forces.[4]

To carry out these orders, MG Rosecrans moved his army south to Union held Nashville, Tennessee in November 1862. After six weeks of reorganization and stockpiling supplies, he moved toward the Confederate Army of Tennessee, commanded by General Braxton Bragg, located 25 miles southeast of Nashville. The Confederates attacked the Union army north of the town of Murfreesboro, along the banks of Stones River, from 31 December 1862 to 2 January 1863. It was a defensive victory for MG Rosecrans, Gen Bragg's offensive power was spent and he was forced to retreat south to the Tullahoma area. When MG Rosecrans and his army crossed Stones River and entered Murfreesboro on 5 January, it marked the beginning of preparations for a new campaign. The new campaign, the Tullahoma, culminated a long six months later with the Confederate forces driven from middle Tennessee and the Army of the Cumberland poised to advance on Chattanooga.[5]

The geography of the Department of the Cumberland is restrictive and had a profound impact on the plans that the army commanders adopted in the Tullahoma campaign. The northern boundary with the Department of the Ohio, as previously mentioned, was the Tennessee-Kentucky state line. The western 20 percent of Tennessee was part of the Department of the Tennessee commanded by MG Ulysses S. Grant. The dividing line was the Tennessee River which runs roughly north/ south across Tennessee. The eastern boundary was the Tennessee/ North Carolina state line. The southern boundary was as far south into Alabama or Georgia as the Union forces needed to go. Within these confines was a varied landscape of creeks, rivers, hills and mountains which would challenge any traveler in 1863, let alone an invading army confronted by a determined foe.

The geography is dominated by two major mountain ranges and two major rivers. The east side of the department is walled in by the Great Smoky Mountains of the Appalachian Range. On their west side they fall into the fertile valley created by the Tennessee River and its tributaries. Passing through this valley, the ground rises 900 feet up the mountain range called the Cumberland Plateau. The top of this range is not capped by peaks but by a flat, sparsely settled, 50 mile wide plateau covered with poor roads, brush, trees, little water and unfit for large scale agriculture. Still heading west, the plateau drops 900 feet into the region known as "The Barrens." It is another sparsely settled area with poor soil and bad roads. Next there is a low range of hills, running around Nashville, called the Highland Rim. These hills have gaps running through them with improved roads linking the towns and villages of the area. Inside the Highland Rim is the region known as the Nashville Basin. This fertile, populated area was some of the best agricultural land in the state. West of the Highland Rim, the flat, fertile land continues unbroken by any mountain ranges to the Tennessee River.[6]

Two major rivers flowed through the department, the Tennessee and the Cumberland, from which the department and army took its name. The Tennessee is created by the French Broad and Clinch Rivers that flow out of the Appalachians and come together near Knoxville, Tennessee. It flows south past Chattanooga near the Georgia border before cutting west through the Cumberland Plateau then across northern Alabama and Mississippi before heading north back into Tennessee. Running on a roughly northern course, it enters Kentucky and empties into the Ohio River at Paducah. The river is navigable to riverboats except at times of low water in the summer which makes passage at Muscle Shoals, Alabama and at a narrow rapids section west of Chattanooga near Williams Island, known as "the Suck," difficult.[7]

The Cumberland River's headwaters lie in the Cumberland Mountains of eastern Kentucky, northeast of the Cumberland Gap. It flows west across southern Kentucky before dipping down into Tennessee. It passes Nashville and then gradually flows northwest back into Kentucky and empties into the Ohio River east of Paducah, not far from where the Tennessee River ends. The Cumberland is also navigable except at times of low water when the Harpeth Shoals, near Clarksville, Tennessee, become a hazard.[8] Both of these rivers were opened to Union river traffic in the winter of 1862 when MG Grant captured Forts Henry and Donelson on the Tennessee and Cumberland Rivers, respectively.[9]

With the major rivers running east to west across the Department of the Cumberland and the Union army needing to drive north to south, the rivers were not viable avenues of invasion, especially with the low water levels of the summer months. Due to the size of the invading armies, an invasion was impossible to manage logistically if only wagons could be used to haul the food, fodder, ammunition for resupply. The major transportation system that could haul the amounts of supplies needed and ran north to south were the railroads of the region, specifically, the Louisville & Nashville Railroad and the Nashville & Chattanooga Railroad. These two rail lines would be the route of invasion for the Army of the Cumberland on its drive to Chattanooga and the sole means of resupply and communications back to the north in the summer and fall of 1863.

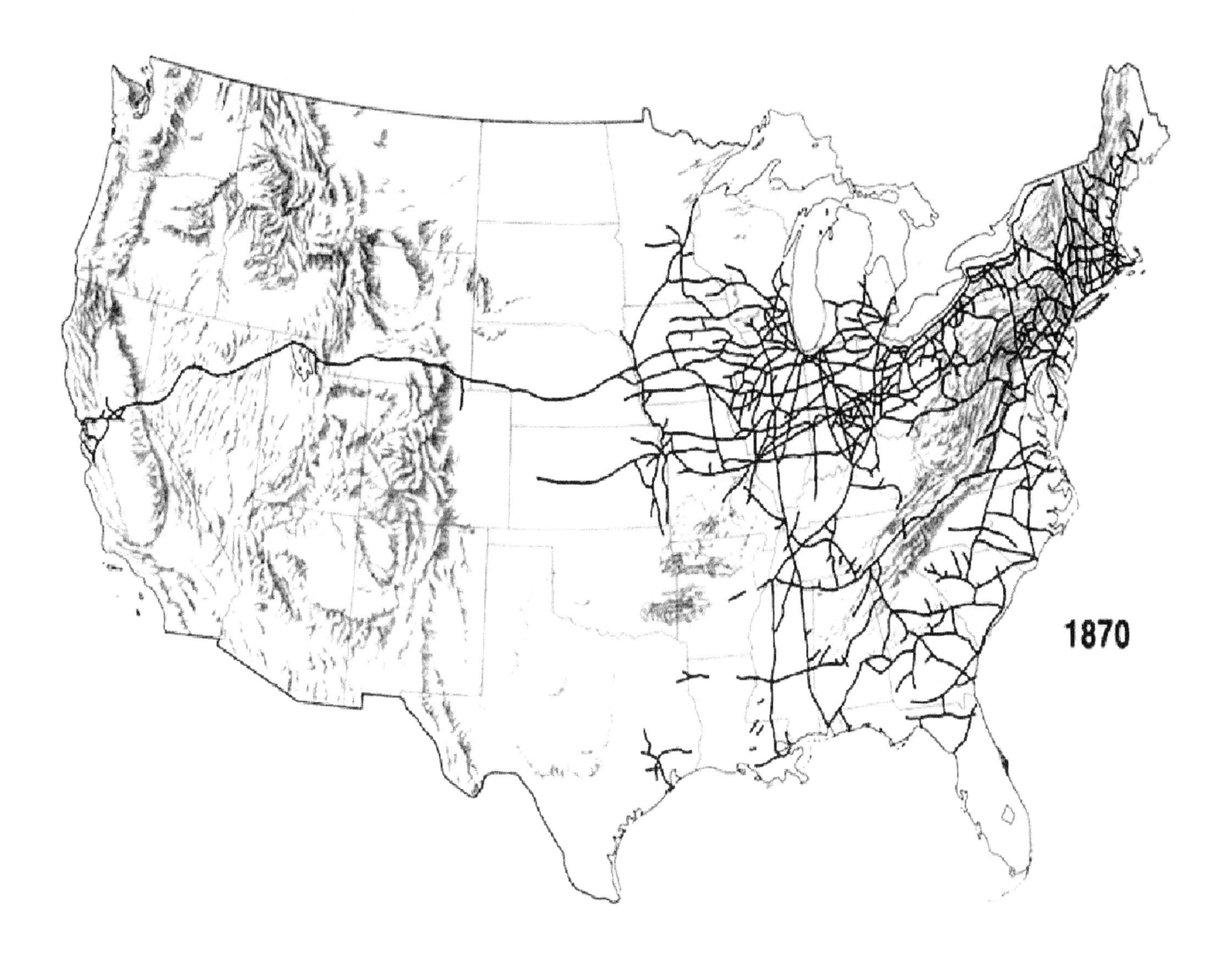

Figure 1. Railroads in and around the Department of the Cumberland
Source: www.nps.gov

The Louisville & Nashville Railroad (L&N) began in 1850 when the Tennessee legislature granted a company charter to build a railroad from Nashville north to Guthrie, Tennessee on the Kentucky state line. The Kentucky legislature then approved a charter for a railroad to be built from Louisville, at the state's northern border on the Ohio River, south to meet up with the line coming out of Nashville. The goal was to free Nashville from dependence on the unreliable Cumberland River for transportation and to ensure Louisville continued being the export-import center for the rich Kentucky tobacco region.[10] It was not until 1855 that the financing of the project was in place and the first rails were laid. The engineers had to overcome numerous obstacles when constructing the roadbed. Muldraugh's Hill near Elizabethtown, Kentucky needed a 1,986-foot tunnel blasted through it and the Green River required the largest iron bridge in the country at the time to span its 1,800 feet. Then, the Barren River and the Tennessee Ridge had to be breached and the South Tunnel near Gallatin, Tennessee had to be blasted before crossing the Cumberland River on a swing-bridge (to allow steam boats to pass) and entering Nashville. These major obstacles, along with dozens of smaller rivers, creeks and cuts, made the line a challenge to build and maintain.[11]

The line was finished under company president James Guthrie, who would head the company throughout the Civil War, in October 1859.[12] (President Guthrie was a former state legislator and US Secretary of the Treasury under Franklin Pierce and would be elected to the US Senate in 1865. His political clout would serve the L&N well throughout the war.[13]) It was a 185-mile-long single-tracked line that was hastily laid down and was lacking ballast, or gravel fill, between the ties over many miles of the line. The biggest problem was the lack of rolling stock available on the line. In 1861, 30 locomotives, 28 passenger cars, and 297 freight cars were owned by the line. Since only a fraction of these would be made available to MG Rosecrans and the rest were used for civilian purposes, shipping in the 500 tons of supplies needed each day by the Army of the Cumberland was very problematic for the quartermasters in 1863.[14]

When the Civil War began, the L&N operated in a tenuous position. Part of it lay in Confederate Tennessee and part in Union Kentucky. While it was lucrative for a time with supplies being shipped south by northern manufacturers, eventually the company suffered under embargos, equipment confiscations, and line destruction. Somehow it managed to survive as a corporation while split between Union and Confederate controlled territory. By October 1862, the Union forces had permanently gained control of the territory up to Nashville. For the rest of the war, the L&N was allowed to operate freely as one continuous rail line, though the retreating Confederates had ravaged it by burning or blowing up bridges over the Salt, Nolin, Green, and Cumberland Rivers and Bacon Creek and burning all the depot buildings at Bowling Green, Kentucky. Much of the previously confiscated rolling stock was recovered but it, along with most of the rail line, was very poorly maintained by the Confederates and needed substantial repairs. [15]

Since this line was allowed to run as an independent business under contract with the government, the company and departments it served, the Ohio and the Cumberland, jointly maintained and operated it with funds and labor.[16] To facilitate this, John B. Anderson, the Superintendent of the L&N, was commissioned a colonel and made Superintendent of Railroads by BG William T. Sherman and retained by MG Buell and then MG Rosecrans.[17] His responsibilities and authority actually covered the full length of the line, and onto the Nashville & Chattanooga, thereby crossing over the two separate military departments and two separate railroads.[18] The Superintendent was to coordinate the efforts of the L&N, the engineer units, and the quartermasters in maintaining and operating the line. COL Anderson had a mixed record of success and was relieved by MG Rosecrans in August 1863. He was reinstated after MG Rosecrans was replaced only to be relieved again for inefficiency by MG Grant. There were also accusations of collusion between COL Anderson and Mr. Guthrie of the L&N, in regard to charging 25 percent higher rates than other railroads and allowing a great deal of civilian freight to be hauled, a more lucrative business for the L&N, which restricted the supplies going to the Army of the Cumberland.[19] This would lead to tighter control by the United States Military Railroad under BG McCallum in 1864-1865.[20]

The lack of rolling stock was partially alleviated in 1862 when the War Department, under the president's new authority, arranged for the transfer of locomotives and freight cars to the L&N from northern railroads. The problem was that most northern roads were becoming standardized at 4-foot and 8 ½-inch gauge and the L&N was a 5-foot gauge track. The northern rolling stock had to be refitted for use south of the Ohio River, and rolling stock was also constructed by the L&N and by contractors.[21] The need was always great due not only to the constant heavy strain on the overused equipment, but also the constant destructive raids on the rail lines by local Confederate guerrilla bands and the cavalry commanders BG John Hunt Morgan, BG Nathan Bedford Forrest, BG Joseph Wheeler, and MG Earl Van Dorn (discussed later in this chapter.)

The Louisville & Nashville connected with the Nashville & Chattanooga (N&C) Railroad after it crossed the Cumberland River and passed through to the west side of Nashville.[22] (This link was built in 1862 to facilitate the passing of freight straight through to points south of Nashville without transferring it to new cars.)[23] The N&C was chartered by the state of Tennessee in 1845 and the company organized in 1848 with Vernon K. Stevenson becoming the first president (the town of Stevenson, Alabama is named for him). The track was built heading south out of Nashville with the first cars traveling as far as Murfreesboro in 1851. From Murfreesboro, it went to Wartrace (with a spur line west to Shelbyville), across the Duck River, then to Tullahoma (where is connected with the McMinnville & Manchester line that headed northeast), over the Elk River to Dechard (where the Winchester & Alabama line would head off to the southwest), until it reached the village of Cowan 87 miles from Nashville. It was there the first major geographic obstacle was met, the steep incline of the Cumberland Plateau. Between 1848 and 1851, a 2,228-foot tunnel was bored through the mountain. Once through the tunnel, the line moved south to the new town of Stevenson, Alabama, the juncture with the Memphis & Charleston Railroad. From there the line headed northeast to the town of Bridgeport to cross the Tennessee River. Bridgeport was originally called Jonesville and was just a river landing with a few houses and stores and a gristmill. The name was changed to Bridgeport in 1854 with the completion of the N&C railroad bridge. It was actually two bridges, a 1,232-foot span to Long Island that lay in the river, and a 428-foot span that reached to the far shore. The bridge was double decked, trains ran on the top deck and wagons on the bottom. Then the line passed through a gap in Sand Mountain to Shellmound, Whiteside, and Wauhatchie, Tennessee, before passing by the northern foot of Lookout Mountain and entering Chattanooga, 151 miles from Nashville. There it linked with the Western & Atlantic Railroad that went south to Atlanta, Georgia and the East Tennessee and Georgia Railroad that headed northeast to Knoxville and Virginia.[24]

When the war began, the N&C lay completely in Confederate territory. Mr. Stevenson, still president of the line, became a major in the Confederate Army serving as the quartermaster in Nashville. As Union forces captured and held larger portions of the line throughout 1862 and 1863, the Union commanders became responsible for maintaining the line since they had no legitimate railroad corporation to contract with. By September 1863, the entire line of the N&C was controlled by the Army of the Cumberland. President Stevenson (he continued on as president even after entering Confederate service), who had moved most of the rolling stock of the company south and leased it to other railroads (forcing rolling stock from the L&N to be used on this line as well), was now in Atlanta and resigned in the summer of 1864 and a new president was named, of neutral sympathies, back in Nashville. The new president could only track costs and damages of the line and its equipment; the company did not regain control of the line until September 1865.[25]

The N&C was the vital link that enabled MG Rosecrans in 1863 (and MG Sherman in 1864) to logistically support his enormous army hundreds of miles into Confederate territory; only it provided a direct route into the heart of the Confederacy. Had the war begun in 1851 instead of 1861, this invasion route would not have existed and the Union armies may never have been able to reach the interior of the South. Technology and an entrepreneurial spirit came together at just the right time in history to make the Tullahoma and Chickamauga Campaigns possible.

So, due to the reliance on the railroads, the logistics system in the Department of the Cumberland started in Louisville, Kentucky. While Cincinnati became a regional supply depot during the war, it was on the Ohio side of the Ohio River. Covington, Kentucky, across from Cincinnati, had a railroad linking it with the south, but it went through Louisville and was of a different gauge than the L&N, so freight had to be transferred to different cars to head south.[26] Because of this, Louisville was the main depot for supplies entering the Department of the Cumberland.

No bridge crossed the Ohio at either Cincinnati or Louisville during the war. All passengers and freight bound for Louisville came in by water, either on a riverboat or on a ferry from across the river at Jeffersonville, Indiana, where the Jeffersonville, Madison, and Indianapolis Railroad ended. Freight had to be unloaded in Jeffersonville, hauled to the docks, placed on a ferry, sent across, loaded back into wagons and sent up to the train depot to be repacked in cars because the railroads did not extend all the way to the water in 1863 and no rail car ferry service existed. The city contained a vast logistical complex to supply the armies to the south. Stables, corrals, wagon and harness shops, quartermaster and ordnance depots, barracks, invalid soldiers home, and two general hospitals were all located there.[27] Quartermasters had the option to ship supplies south by either riverboat or rail, but as previously discussed, the river systems were unreliable in the summer months. It must be remembered that the Department of the Ohio troops in the interior of Kentucky, a great many of whom were detailed to defend the rail line itself, also relied on the L&N for resupply, and the L&N was still allowed to handle civilian freight and passengers. So MG Rosecrans' army was competing for space on the limited rolling stock coming into his department. This became so problematic in September 1863 that the L&N was only allocating 16 carloads of freight for the army to travel south to Stevenson when 60 were required. This was a deciding factor in the USMRR taking control of the line in 1864, though lack of rolling stock, poor maintenance, and high rates also contributed. Sadly, reforms only happened after the defeat at Chickamauga.[28]

The Chief Quartermaster of the Western District, the link between the Quartermaster Bureau in Washington and the departmental quartermasters operating in western Virginia, Kentucky, and Tennessee, was COL Thomas Swords.[29] He operated the depots in Louisville and Cincinnati throughout the Tullahoma and Chickamauga Campaigns.[30] His quartermaster officers and civilian clerks gathered the supplies in Louisville from national, regional and local contractors and arranged for the transportation of all the goods south, to include ordnance, commissary and medical stores from their local depots. The officer that ran the Louisville quartermaster depot for COL Swords was Captain Walworth Jenkins.[31] When the telegraph and rail lines were operational, an order could be sent to Louisville and within four days the supplies could be in Stevenson, Alabama.[32]

As the L&N headed south, towns along its path were built up as depots for the troops guarding the line and patrolling for guerrillas in the area. Elizabethtown, Munfordville, and Bowling Green, Kentucky and Gallatin, Tennessee became prominent stations to support these troops.[33]

Upon the freight reaching Nashville, the gangs of laborers hired by the quartermasters could unload the freight and the local quartermaster, ordnance, commissary and medical staffs could transport the goods to their rented warehouses near the train depots or the riverfront, or the goods could immediately be sent farther south.[34] The chief quartermaster in Nashville, Captain (CPT) Henry C. Hodges, was ultimately responsible for finding storage space and arranging transportation in and out of Nashville. Dr. Robert Fletcher was the medical purveyor, or purchasing officer, for the Department of the Cumberland. He operated out of Nashville as did the chief commissary officer,

CPT Samuel J. Little, and the chief of ordnance, CPT Edwin Townsend.[35] Nashville, and all the depots along the L&N and N&C, was ringed with forts and trenches to protect the supplies stored there and the depots in Tennessee were garrisoned by a division of the Army of the Cumberland whose commander during the summer of 1863 was BG Robert S. Granger of the Reserve Corps.[36]

MG Rosecrans had his own logistics staff that had dual roles as both the Department and the Army of the Cumberland logisticians. The logisticians on his staff had regular army commissions and were provided to MG Rosecrans by their respective bureaus in Washington. They were the senior logisticians in the field but depot chiefs answered to both the field army logisticians and the regional chief back in Louisville/ Cincinnati.

The Army of the Cumberland's Chief Quartermaster was Lieutenant Colonel (LTC) John W. Taylor. The son of a former Speaker of the US House of Representatives and pre-war businessman in Illinois and Iowa, LTC Taylor became the chief quartermaster in MG John Pope's Army of the Mississippi in 1862. He served in the same capacity under MG Rosecrans when he commanded that army and MG Rosecrans brought him over to the Army of the Cumberland when he was transferred. He was a capable man but one that was not well liked by his subordinates.[37] The quartermasters under his supervision organized foraging expeditions into the countryside each day to gather forage for the horses and mules, hired laborers for the rail yards, had barracks and warehouses built, purchased supplies for the railroad, coordinated with the rail lines for shipments, tracked supplies issued, rented and refurbished buildings to serve as hospitals, and made projections as to future consumption rates. He also had to keep the army supplied with and maintain the 2,411 wagons and 13,877 mules (as reported by the corps' in their monthly inspection reports that will be discussed later) that carried the food and ammunition of the army in the field.[38] It was a varied and never ending mission executed with too few officers with too little rank.

LTC Samuel Simmons was the Chief Commissary for the army. A lawyer in civilian life, he had been a commissary officer since entering the army. He was also an Army of the Mississippi transferee.[39] LTC Simmons was unable to gather much in the way of foodstuffs from the surrounding countryside; the armies stationed in the region in the past year had picked it clean. Most of the commissary stores had to be shipped south on the railroad and river (which was used extensively throughout the winter and spring even with Confederate cavalry and guerrilla attacks forcing steamships into convoys with gunboat escorts). He also had some diverse commodities under his responsibilities; for example, he had to provide all the candles the army used.[40]

The Chief of Ordnance for the army was CPT Horace Porter. An 1860 graduate of West Point, he had already seen a great deal of the war while serving at the bombardment of Fort Pulaski, Georgia, with the Army of the Potomac, and the Army of the Ohio. CPT Porter was assigned as the ordnance chief in January 1863. (Later, he would impress MG Grant during the Chattanooga Campaign. MG Grant brought him onto his personal staff and Porter would end the war a BG.)[41]

CPT Porter's greatest challenge was supplying the proper amount of ammunition to the varied caliber weapons in the army. The army had thirteen models of rifles and muskets, nine different calibers of cartridges, and twenty-five sizes of artillery shells, and a variety of accoutrements assigned to its units and soldiers.[42] CPT Porter was praised in

MG Rosecrans' report of the Chickamauga Campaign for his efforts in arming each regiment with the same caliber weapons, thereby simplifying the ammunition resupply on the battlefield. With approximately 67,000 soldiers in the field in the summer of 1863, CPT Porter was responsible for providing a basic load of 60 rounds and a resupply from the army's 375 (25 authorized per division, multiplied by 15 divisions) division ordnance wagons for each soldier or 8,040,000 rounds of rifle and musket ammunition.[43] There were 42 artillery batteries also with varied ammunition needs. There were seven different caliber of cannons with the army and some six-gun batteries had three different caliber guns assigned to them.[44] As discussed in Chapter 2, there were four ammunition chests per gun, so 128 rounds traveled with a 12-pounder and 200 rounds with a 3-inch ordnance or 10-pounder Parrott, for example. The ordnance wagon trains tried to carry an amount equal to that carried with each gun. There was a variety of different types of ammunition carried: solid shot, shell, spherical case, and canister. The fact that no shortages were reported in basic loads of any units prior to going to battle in the summer and fall of 1863 shows CPT Porter's diligence in his duty performance.[45]

The Medical Director for the Army of the Cumberland was Surgeon Glover Perin. Dr. Perin was an 1846 graduate of the Ohio Medical School with 16 years of experience as a Regular Army surgeon. He was assigned to the army in February 1863.[46] Dr. Perin found that the army's medical system was "in deplorable condition" and he started reforms within weeks of his arrival. He sought to implement the Letterman System from the Army of the Potomac in the Army of the Cumberland but it would take until January 1864 for it to be fully adopted and supplied throughout the army; the army would be in a state of transition throughout the Tullahoma and Chickamauga Campaigns. He did get

MG Rosecrans to standardize the ambulance system. One ambulance was assigned to each regiment, 10 additional ambulances were assigned to each brigade, and an enlisted ambulance master controlled the use of these ambulances while the quartermasters were responsible for their maintenance. Both the quartermasters and the ambulance masters answered to the corps, division, or brigade medical directors in regards to the use of these vehicles.[47]

There was already a system in place for treating wounded. The regiments and brigades had aid depots set up in their camps or behind the fighting line and the divisions had field hospitals. This was standard across the army except in the Cavalry Corps which had no hospitals. Supporting these field hospitals were field hospitals set up in forward depots and general hospitals in larger cities, the closest being in Nashville.[48] By June 1863, more than 20 general hospitals had been set up by the quartermasters in Nashville and operated by Medical Department staff. These were set up in churches and warehouses and one was built, the Cumberland Hospital which could accommodate 3,000 patients. (The general hospitals answered to the Medical Bureau in Washington, though Dr. Perin had influence over them as the Department Medical Director.)[49] There were also five passenger railcars set up for medical evacuation of patients. Engines used to move these cars each had their smoke stacks painted scarlet red and three lanterns hung beneath their headlights at night to identify them to guerrilla bands and cavalry raiders. Two of them could transfer up to 60 litter patients at a time. Dr. Perin was also able to improve sanitation and medical care in the camps so that the disease rate per 1,000 soldiers dropped 9.6 percent from 1862 to 1863.[50] While the medical system for the

Army of the Cumberland was not as good as it could have been, it was improving thanks to Dr. Perin's efforts.

The threat of cavalry and guerrilla raids on the railroads was significant and played a major role in all campaigns that took place in middle Tennessee, both before, during and after MG Rosecrans' time in command there. In February 1862, MG Buell's Army of the Ohio had advanced into Nashville and captured the length of the L&N, but this single tracked line was extremely vulnerable. It was very easy for cavalry units, guerrilla bands, and even individuals to pull up rails, burn bridges, depots and water towers, cut telegraph wire, and effectively cut the lines of communication and supply for the Union army deep in Confederate territory. The L& N board immediately organized crews to begin repairs on the badly damaged line. But on 15 March, BG John Hunt Morgan made his first of many raids on the L&N. He entered Gallatin, Tennessee that day and destroyed a workcrew train consisting of an engine and 13 cars. Two months later he entered Cave City, Kentucky and attacked two trains destroying 37 freight and 3 passenger cars.[51]

In May 1862, MG Halleck led an army group, which included MG Buell's army, from Pittsburg Landing, Tennessee to the rail junction at Corinth, Mississippi. He then dispersed his armies with MG Buell's force being sent east along the Memphis & Charleston (M&C) Railroad to Bridgeport, Alabama. BG Ormsby Mitchel's division already occupied the section from Decatur to Stevenson, Alabama and MG Buell was to reinforce his gains and rebuild the railroad up to Bridgeport on the Tennessee. The goal was to drive east to Chattanooga using the M&C as his main resupply line.[52] To prepare for this Stevenson, Alabama, the junction of the M&C and N&C, became a forward depot. MG Buell believed that the line coming south should be his main logistical route and keeping it and the route to the west open stretched his meager resources too far; he could neither repair nor protect both tracks at once. He decided to put his efforts into repairing the N&C and had it reopened and working on 12 July. It stayed operational for only one day. On the 13th, BG Nathan Bedford Forrest entered Murfreesboro, Tennessee and captured 1,400 prisoners, a large wagon train, and all the stores in the depot. He also tore up several miles of track. At the same time, BG Morgan's raiders hit the L&C at Lebanon, Kentucky capturing the garrison and burning the stores at the depot. It would be two weeks before the lines were operational again.

Then on 12 August BG Morgan attacked Gallatin, Tennessee capturing the garrison, and destroying a 29-car train, the water station and two bridges in the area. He also attacked Tunnel Hill, Tennessee and captured the garrison as well as burning the support timbers in the tunnel. The destroyed tunnel kept the railroad closed until 25 November, which forced MG Buell to place his soldiers on half rations. The officer responsible for protecting the N&C told MG Buell that it would take 500,000 men to protect the railroad. These raids were a hindrance to MG Buell, but it was GEN Bragg's invasion of Kentucky, which started in Chattanooga, that made MG Buell abandon the forward positions in Bridgeport on 31 August (where he partially burned the bridge over the river) and pull back to Nashville.[53]

During the Murfreesboro Campaign, BG Morgan was sent north to raid MG Rosecrans' newly opened supply line. He hit the line at Glasgow, Kentucky and for a week headed north, tearing up track and burning infrastructure as he went. This destruction, and the inclement weather in January, would keep the line down until 1

February 1863.[54] The line would stay open with only short interruptions from guerrilla activity until 4 July 1863 when BG Morgan attacked Lebanon, Kentucky one last time burning cars, bridges and buildings. (He then headed north and was captured in Ohio and imprisoned, playing no further role in the campaign for Chattanooga.) During the fiscal year ending 30 June 1863, the L&N was only able to operate over its full line for seven months and 12 days.[55]

These and numerous other attacks on wagon trains and rail lines in Tennessee and Kentucky made a big impression on MG Rosecrans and his logistical staff. They also took note of the raid by Confederate MG Earl Van Dorn on MG Grant's logistical base in Holly Springs, Mississippi on 20 December 1862. The capture and destruction of this important base made MG Grant abandon his advance on Vicksburg from the north. It was the only time in the war that a cavalry raid determined the outcome of a campaign.[56] The distance from Louisville and the threat of raids forced MG Rosecrans to dedicate important resources to protecting his supply lines as opposed to using them to drive ahead to Chattanooga.

The protective measures took several forms. MG Rosecrans ordered that blockhouse forts be constructed at all the railroad bridges in the department. These were garrisoned with troops who could defend the bridges and act as a reaction force along their sector of the line. Seven blockhouses would be built between Nashville and Murfreesboro during the winter and spring of 1863 and 47 would eventually be built between Nashville and Chattanooga.[57] MG Rosecrans also decided to build a new forward logistical depot just north of Murfreesboro. To defend it, he built a massive 200-acre fort that overlapped the Nashville Pike, N&C rail line, and Stones River. It was started in January and, with 4,000 men working on it each day, was completed in June 1863 and named Fortress Rosecrans. When completed, the fort was large enough to protect an army of 50,000 men, and could stockpile enough supplies to feed the army for 90 days. It contained four sawmills, a 50-acre vegetable garden, a field hospital, and quartermaster, commissary and ordnance depots.[58] The intent for building it was not to house a huge army, but to protect the supplies of the army from raids with minimal troops. This would free up soldiers for the field campaign in the summer. Six platform cars were also outfitted as train guard cars with thick planking up the sides and seats for the guards to ride on and fire from.[59]

Being able to quickly rebuild the destroyed rail line and support buildings was a key to keeping any forward momentum in the summer campaign. To do this, MG Rosecrans needed engineers and experienced construction crews. The sole engineering unit in his department when he took it over was the 1st Michigan Engineers & Mechanics. It was raised by COL William P. Innes of Grand Rapids, Michigan in 1861; he and his field grade officers and company commanders were all engineers. COL Innes was employed as a railroad construction engineer prior to the war. The fact this regiment was the largest coming out of Michigan, with over 3,200 men serving in it throughout the war, showed the importance it had to the army; replacements were funneled to it instead of to infantry or cavalry units. It normally worked in three separate battalions, each commanded by one of the field grade officers or a senior company commander.[60] Since the maintenance and repair of the railroad, along with the numerous other engineering and construction duties of the engineers, could not be done by this one unit of less than 1,000 men, MG Rosecrans created a Pioneer Brigade. He got the idea from BG Grenville

Dodge who created a similar unit in June 1862 to rebuild the Mobile & Ohio Railroad in Mississippi.[61] MG Rosecrans had detailed 20 men (half "mechanics" and half laborers) from each regiment in the army. The 2,000 detailed men (the number fluctuated) were grouped together in three battalions and brigaded together under the command of newly promoted BG James St. Clair Morton, the Chief Engineer for the Army of the Cumberland. The Pioneer Brigade trained on road repair, fortification construction and bridge building, to include emplacing a new 700-foot pontoon bridge.[62] These two units would be busy before the campaign season preparing defenses, building warehouses, and improving the rail line and would travel with the corps as they moved forward during the campaigns to repair the roads and railroads the Union troops were using.

The final countermeasure to the Confederate raids that MG Rosecrans put in place, and the one that caused the greatest controversy with his superiors, was his vast expansion of the cavalry in the Army of the Cumberland. Following the Battle of Murfreesboro, Secretary of War Stanton told MG Rosecrans, "There is nothing within my power to grant yourself or your heroic command that will not be cheerfully given."[63] With this statement from the Secretary and the realization of the difficult task before him, MG Rosecrans began asking for a great deal of logistical and manpower support.

In response to his request for reinforcements, 14,000 men in two divisions under MG Gordon Granger were sent to him from the Department of the Ohio, including four cavalry regiments.[64] MG Rosecrans had his staff officers ask for large orders of clothing, tools, medical stores, livestock, commissary items, forage, wagons, tents, and especially weapons and mounts for cavalry soldiers and the accoutrements to outfit them. By March 1863, one half million pounds of supplies were arriving in Nashville by rail and river each day for the Army of the Cumberland which enabled a three months worth of supply to be accumulated there and in Murfreesboro.[65] MG Rosecrans was asking for so much in such a short amount of time that his numerous telegrams prompted MG Halleck to lecture him about, "the enormous expense to the Government of your telegrams; more than that of all the other generals in the field."[66]

The cavalry under MG Buell was poorly organized and led and greatly outnumbered by their southern opponents. In November 1862 it numbered about 2,500 men; the Confederate cavalry force was four times its size. To run his cavalry division, MG Rosecrans had BG David S. Stanley transferred from the Department of the Tennessee.[67] While he was not at the same ability level as a Forrest, Morgan, Wheeler or Van Dorn, BG Stanley did effectively oversee a great improvement in the organization, training, size and equipment of the cavalry division.

Four brigades of cavalry were organized following Stones River. Some units were already with the army, while others were transferred in from other departments, like the ones that arrived with MG Granger. Since there was only authorization for a division of cavalry, the brigades were numbered the 1st through the 4th. By May 1863, the War Department had seen the need for an organized cavalry corps and authorized MG Rosecrans to create one. BG Stanley was promoted to MG and he had two divisions, of two brigades each (1st Division would have three by Chickamauga), led by BG's Robert B. Mitchell and George Crook.[68]

Along with the requests for more cavalry soldiers were requests for weapons to arm them. MG Rosecrans wanted breech loading, repeating, and revolving carbines for his cavalry units, the idea being that when armed this way they would still be able to compete with greater numbers of Confederate cavalry.[69] On 30 January 1862, he telegraphed another request, this one for 2,500 breechloaders or revolving carbines.[70] In response, MG Halleck telegraphed him on 1 February;

> You have already more than your share of the best arms. Everything has been done, and is being done, for you that is possible by the Government. Your complaints are without reason. You cannot expect to have all the best arms. The Government cannot give them. Your cavalry is already as well armed as that of Grant or Curtis.

MG Rosecrans arrogantly responded on 2 February, "I do not complain. I point the way to victory." [71] He also lectured Secretary Stanton on 2 February that:

> I speak for the country when I say that 2,000 effective cavalry will cost the support of . . . $5,000 per day. The power of these men will be doubled by good arms. Thus would be saved $5,000 per day. . . . One rebel cavalryman takes on an average of 3 of our infantry to watch our communications while our progress is made slow and cautious. We command the forage of the country only by sending large train guards. It is of prime necessity in every point of view to master their cavalry. . . . We now have 1,000 cavalrymen without horses and 2,000 without arms.[72]

MG Halleck responded on 3 February, "Your telegrams have been couched in terms implying a censure upon the Government for not properly supplying you with cavalry and cavalry arms. You are certainly under a grave misapprehension."[73] This was the beginning of numerous conflicts between MG Rosecrans and the leadership back in the War Department in regards to supplies and lack of forward progress.

Examples of further requests were 5,000 Sharps carbines on 26 March, 6,000 Colt pistols on 30 March, 3,000 sabres on 1 April.[74] One request would be filled and, frustratingly, another immediately came in, displaying a clear lack of planning on the part of MG Rosecrans. The quartermasters and the ordnance officers would make Herculean efforts for the Army of the Cumberland but it was never enough for MG Rosecrans.

The arms of the cavalry would be greatly improved by the start of the Tullahoma Campaign. The idea that COL Wilder's famous mounted infantry brigade was the only mounted force in the army with repeating or breechloading weapons is untrue. For example, by April 1863, the 1st Brigade of the Cavalry Division had 1,568 men present for duty (no listing for numbers absent or sick but it must have been several hundred men) with a total of 1,678 carbines on hand (a mix of Burnside, Gallagher, Merrill, and Colt weapons) and 64 required, and 1,643 pistols on hand (a mix of Savage, Adams, French, Colt, Remington and Whitney weapons) with 365 needed. Each regiment had only one or two makes of a carbine, which eased resupply planning, but could have multiple types of pistols. The 1st Brigade is representative of all four brigades of the division. By the end of May, the last reporting period before the Tullahoma Campaign began in June, the new Cavalry Corps had 7,593 men present for duty with 6,638 carbines on hand and 371 required (the discrepancy in numbers present and numbers of carbines on hand and needed must be due to not counting officers as needing carbines.)[75] So all but a few hundred cavalry had breech loading or repeating carbines when the Tullahoma campaign began. COL Wilder had an advantage in his brigade as to the uniformity of his rifles, but the Cavalry Corps was armed with the best carbines the North had to offer.

The other problem with the cavalry troops was keeping them mounted. MG Rosecrans telegraphed MG Halleck on 17 April:

> I repeat what I have often said, the true objective for us being the enemy's forces, not locality, our fundamental want is mounted forces sufficient to control the country, and, in case we beat them, to follow and destroy them. I have been urgent in asking for horses since October last. We have 3,500 dismounted cavalry.[76]

This same day he ordered MG Stanley to go to Louisville with all his dismounted troops (he only took 1,000) to speed up the process of finding them mounts.[77] On 20 April MG Halleck telegraphed that, "you have telegraphed at least a dozen, and, perhaps, twenty times in the last few months that you require more cavalry" and these constant requests are "injuring you in the estimation of the government."[78] MG Rosecrans sent Secretary Stanton a telegram on 24 April saying, yet again, how much he needed cavalry horses and that his force was only at 40 percent strength at any one time due to the lack of mounts.[79]

Since he was going nowhere with the General-in-Chief and the Secretary of War, MG Rosecrans began telegraphing the man whose bureau was responsible for purchasing and transporting the horses, Quartermaster General Meigs. Since MG Rosecrans was complaining about the number of bad horses being supplied him, BG Meigs asked that MG Rosecrans detail cavalry officers to assist his quartermaster officers in Louisville with the inspection of horses provided by contractors, which was done.[80]

Now that BG Meigs was being pulled into the situation, he began doing the math on the numbers of horses and mules supplied to MG Rosecrans. He had MG Halleck request on 25 April, a total count of what MG Rosecrans thought he had received and what he had on hand since taking over command.[81] On 27 April MG Rosecrans responded:

> This army had, December 1, 1862, 8,709 horses and 11,519 mules, received from the Department of the Ohio. Procured by capture or purchase since, 18,450 horses and 14,607 mules. Sent off, unserviceable, 9,119 horses and 1,149 mules. On hand, March 23, 19,164 horses and 23,859 mules. . . . It is reported by the chief quartermaster that one-third of the animals now on hand are used up and unserviceable.[82]

After additional telegrams to BG Meigs from MG Rosecrans complaining about quartermasters setting the prices for horses too low to get good ones (incorrect since the contracting companies set the prices with bids) and stating that with 10,000 or 20,000 more cavalry he could control all the forage and foodstuffs in middle Tennessee[83], BG Meigs wrote a long letter on 1 May to MG Rosecrans lecturing him on his inaccurate reporting, unrealistic requests, and improperly caring for the animals entrusted to his care:

> Lieutenant Colonel Taylor reports 11,478 cavalry and 3,339 artillery horses on hand on 31st March, say 12,000 mounted men. You say the mounted rebels outnumbered you five to one, and this I do not take to be a careless expression, fore I find it repeatedly used in your dispatches. Have they 60,000 mounted men? How do they find food for them? . . . I cannot but think you are mistaken in your estimate. . . . You report to General Halleck that you have received, since December 1, 18,450 horses and 14,607 mules- 33,057 animals; nearly 7,000 animals per month. Is this not a large supply?... The animals cost, by the time they reach you, nearly $4,000,000. You had on hand March 23, 19,164 horses and 23,859 mules- 43,023 animals in all; or . . . about one horse or mule for every two men in your army. You have broken down and sent off as unserviceable, in addition to these, over 9,000 horses, and report that one-fourth or one-third of the horses on hand are worn out. Now, all this, it seems to me, shows that the horses are not properly treated. They are either overworked, or underfed, or neglected and abused. . . . See what forces you ask for. You have 12,000; you should have 22,000 or 32,000 mounted men. Had it been possible to furnish so many men with horses, it would have been necessary to furnish more horses still to transport forage for these, and the difficulty of feeding them would have been greater and greater. I doubt the wisdom of building up such masses, which crumble under their own weight. . . . [T]his long inactivity tells severely upon the resources of the country.[84]

MG Rosecrans responded on 10 May trying to refute BG Meigs' letter in regard to the numbers of horses, but the numbers he presented did not match with what he wrote earlier (total of 9,359 horses on hand of which 2,028 were orderlies and escorts).[85]

To reduce the numbers of detailed cavalry and horses, MG Rosecrans issued General Order No. 113 on 17 May. It stated that brigades could only have one NCO and

4 privates mounted as orderlies at the headquarters and division headquarters were allowed one NCO and 9 privates, and that all vedettes and patrols would be controlled by the cavalry corps.[86] MG Rosecrans still did not let up with his demands to Washington for cavalry; on 21 May he stated that with 6,000 more cavalry he would attack within three days, but without them it would be too hazardous.[87]

No matter what may have been debated at the higher levels in the army, the Cavalry Corps reported in the May inspection report 7,593 cavalrymen present with 6,105 horses serviceable, 853 unserviceable (an unspecific categorization, usually just needed rest, food and a dry corral to recover) and a need of 913.[88] So by late June 1863, MG Rosecrans had roughly 7,000 cavalry with excellent arms and a horse to mount for operations against the estimated 13,000 Confederate cavalrymen in the Army of Tennessee.[89]

Since he was having difficulty in getting cavalry units assigned to him, MG Rosecrans asked for and received permission to mount infantry units to augment his cavalry. On 16 February 1863, he issued Special Field Order Number 44 authorizing COL John T. Wilder's infantry brigade of MG George Thomas' XIV Corps to become a mounted infantry brigade. Thirty-two year old COL Wilder operated an iron foundry in Indiana before the war. He had been commissioned as a captain in the 17th Indiana Infantry in 1861 and by 1863 had risen to regimental and then brigade command. COL Wilder had asked permission to mount his unit after an unsuccessful tour guarding the L&N railroad when he could not catch the Confederate raiders that attacked his section of the line. The intent was to use them as dragoons, or infantrymen who rode horses to a fight but dismounted during the fight. To outfit the brigade, the quartermasters provided horses and the brigade itself also patrolled the countryside around Nashville and

Murfreesboro confiscating horses and providing promissory notes for payment. They also needed to be outfitted with harnesses, saddles, wagons, etc by the quartermasters to make them functional. By April the approximately 1,500-man brigade was mounted and ready to take the field.[90]

COL Wilder sought to outfit his mounted infantrymen with repeating rifles to increase their power on the battlefield. Initially he wanted Henry rifles but, after seeing a demonstration by Christopher Spencer in the spring of 1863, he received permission to arm his soldiers with seven shot Spencer rifles. The Ordnance Bureau would not purchase the rifles for the unit so COL Wilder decided he would buy them himself and the men would gradually pay him back the $35 cost each month from their salaries. But the Government intervened and paid for the carbines before any soldier's pay was deducted. The carbines arrived in June and the brigade was armed and ready for the Tullahoma Campaign to begin. Wilder's Brigade would not work for the Cavalry Corps but stayed in MG Thomas' XIV Corps and worked for 4th Division commander BG Joseph J. Reynolds during the Tullahoma Campaign; he would be on detached duty during the Chickamauga Campaign.[91] This made resupply and command and control difficult since the brigade was essentially used as a cavalry force but, being separate from the normal cavalry supply channels, required special considerations within MG Thomas' infantry corps. The unit would gain fame during Tullahoma and Chickamauga for its actions and earn the nickname "The Lightning Brigade," so MG Rosecrans' efforts to increase his mounted forces did pay off for the army. MG McCook's XX Corps also had mounted infantry but only one regiment, the 39th Indiana under COL T.J. Harrison. They too were issued Spencer rifles and made a reputation for themselves in the campaigns in scouting and reconnaissance. The number of soldiers in the regiment is not readily available, but with the average size of a Civil War regiment being 350 men, it is reasonable to assume it numbered at least this many though it probably had many more since it had the winter and spring to recruit new members.[92] (Another infantry brigade, under COL Abel Streight, was mounted on mules [requiring less forage] to attempt a raid on the Confederate supply line in north Georgia. COL Streight and 1,600 of his men were captured by BG Forrest in May 1863.)[93]

As mentioned in Chapter 2, once units obtained wagons to haul its supplies and "luxuries" in the field, it was difficult to get them to part with them. MG Rosecrans found his units loaded down with excess wagons which slowed down his rate of march and required enormous resources to maintain and fodder and forage to feed the mule teams. Because of this, he issued several orders to reduce the number of wagons in his corps. On 3 February, Special Field Order Number 31 said each infantry regiment could have 10 wagons; each cavalry regiment was allowed 25 wagons; each battery could have a wagon for each gun; each brigade headquarters was allowed five wagons; and each division also got 25 wagons for ammunition and another 40 for supplies. All excess wagons were to be turned into the depot at Nashville.[94]

On 16 February, General Order Number 21 further specified that each division headquarters was allowed seven wagons, the headquarters for each regiment could have one wagon; the medical department could have one wagon per regiment; that each wagon would be plainly marked on the body of the wagon which company and regiment it belonged to; and that on the march, each company wagon would hold three days rations for the men and four days rations for the animals.[95]

The number of tents being used by the army also concerned MG Rosecrans because they were both expensive and filled up the wagons. So on 12 April, he issued General Order Number 78, which allowed one wall tent per brigade, division or corps headquarters; one wall tent for every two officers of the staffs; three wall tents for the officers of each regiment; two hospital tents per regiment (to house sick and store supplies); one wall tent for the men of each company (unless supplied with shelter or "pup" tents); and each tent was to be plainly marked with the regiment to which it belonged.[96]

MG Rosecrans was apparently not seeing the number of wagons reduced because he felt compelled to issue General Orders Number 104 on 8 May in an attempt to reduce the amount of baggage the army had accumulated in its long stay in Nashville and Murfreesboro. It stated that general officers could have 125 pounds of baggage; field grade officers were allowed 100 pounds; and company grade officers were allowed 80 pounds. Non-commissioned officers and privates baggage (both worn and in the knapsack) would consist of one blanket, two pairs of drawers, two pairs of socks, one jacket or blouse, one pair of trousers, one pair of shoes or boots, and one hat or cap, and "none other". Any soldier found straggling would have their knapsack inspected and any extra clothing would be "immediately thrown out."[97]

Comparing consolidated monthly reports for the Army of the Cumberland prior to the summer campaigns will allow an analysis of the logistical strength of the army and its compliance to MG Rosecrans' directives (see table 1):

Table 1. January Inspection Report				
23 January '63	XIV Corps	XX Corps	XXI Corps	Total
Men (Officers + Enlisted present)-	26,045	14,045	11,689	51,779
Tents-	4,195	2,425	1,801	8,421
Wagons-	701	417	541	1,659
Ambulances-	142	107	86	335
Horses*-	1,202	668	700	2,570
Mules-	3,427	2,033	2,631	8,091

*These totals apparently do not count artillery horses. A corps with three divisions, with 3 brigades in each division, with one battery per brigade, and each gun having six horses pulling it and six pulling its caisson, would mean 72 horses per 6 gun battery and 648 artillery horses in the entire corps.

In the May report, the new two-man shelter, or "pup," tents had been issued greatly expanding the number of tents (see table 2):

Table 2. May Inspection Report						
May '63*	XIV Corps	XX Corps	XXI Corps	1st MI E&M	PIO. BDE	Total
Men (Officers + Enlisted present)-	29,537	15,921	14,285	719	2,190	62,652
Tents-	16,823	8,857	8,048	109	1,141	34,978
Wagons-	1,056	548	479	36	41	2,160
Ambulances-	152	113	NA (86 in Jan.)	NA	NA	351
Horses-	3,492**	754	411	68	92	4,817
Mules-	6,000	3,383	2,562	80	214	12,239

*BG Garfield stated on 12 June that 15,050 soldiers were guarding the supply line north of Murfreesboro to the Tennessee state line and unavailable for active campaigning.[98]

**COL Wilder's Brigade was in XIV Corps, but his brigade which numbered only around 1,500, does not account for so many horses in the corps. Artillery horses may be included.

MG Rosecrans was given permission to create a new corps and on 8 June issued Special Field Order 156 that transferred the Fourth Division of the XIV Corps to MG

Gordon Granger's command. This new division, coupled with the two divisions he brought with him from the Army of Kentucky, became MG Granger's Reserve Corps.[99] Since the Army of the Cumberland did not have consolidated inspection reports for June 1863, due to the ongoing Tullahoma Campaign (the same would be true in August when the Chickamauga campaign began) and no large-scale battles took place so few men became casualties and little equipment was destroyed or captured, the July report will have to be used to show the men and equipment in the army for the Tullahoma and Chickamauga Campaigns. The new Cavalry Corps reported in May for the first time. Its report is not available for July so the May numbers have been reused in order to include the entire army. Also, there was a new form used to tabulate the equipment so a more detailed look at the tentage is available (see table 3):

How well did the Army of the Cumberland comply with MG Rosecrans' directives? The directive dealing with tents was complied with. The enlisted men had shelter tents issued to them, the 35,949 shelter tents being enough for over 70,000 men, excluding the cavalry whose numbers are unavailable. The number of hospital tents and wall tents does match the number of regimental officers and regiments (using 37 per). With 170 infantry regiments in the army and two hospital tents allowed per regiment, the army was under its 340 authorized with only 174. It can be assumed this deficit would be made up by the variety of Sibley, Bell, and Common tents in the inventory. The Reserve Corps is the exception; they had great many more tents than the other corps, though this is undoubtedly due to two of its divisions not being fully

Table 3. July Inspection Report*							
31 July '63	XIV Corps	XX Corps	XXI Corps	Res. Corps	Cav. Corps	Detached Cmds	Total
Men (Officers + Enlisted)-	26,160 present + 8,894 absent 35,054 total	13,894 present + 8,260 absent 22,154 total	16,129 present + 6,794 absent 22,923 total	18,747 present + 14,467 absent 33,214 total	7,593 present + NA 7,593 total	3,022 present + 1,176 absent 4,198 total	85,545 present + 39,591 absent 125,136 total
Wagons-	725	375	470	412	356	73	2,411
Ambulances-	132	63	70	43	27	8	343
Horses**-	561***	799****	511	493	6,958	190	9,512
Mules-	4,359	2,186	2,676	2,413	1,858	385	13,877
Tents*****-							
Hospital-	52	31	42	44	NA	5	174
Sibley-	24	19	9	197	NA	0	249
Wall-	628	224	421	643	NA	70	1,986
Bell-	31	2	34	448	NA	82	597
Common-	5	3	2	170	NA	1	181
Shelter-	13,294	6,273	8,204	7,240	NA	938	35,949

*1st Michigan Engineers & Mechanics and Pioneer Brigade numbers unavailable.

**The total number of artillery horses for the 252 guns in 42 batteries (pulling two limbers with each gun) in the army must have numbered 3,024. COL Wilder additionally carried four smaller mountain howitzers broken down on mules with his battery.

***COL Wilder's Brigade horses not listed in this report. If they were, approximately 1,500 horses would be added. These and the artillery horses together with those in the inspection report would total 15,536 horses in the Army of the Cumberland.

****39th Indiana Mounted Infantry not included, at least 350 more horses to total.

*****Value of showing tents is to illustrate equipment losses following Chickamauga.

incorporated into the Army of the Cumberland until June; they must have still been operating under the old Army of Kentucky standards.

The issue of number of wagons is different. The total number of wagons listed the inspection reports equals 2,411. But MG Rosecrans' orders authorized the army to have a total of 5,092 wagons (see table 4):

Table 4. Summer 1863 Wagon Authorizations							
Summer '63*	XIV Corps	XX Corps	XXI Corps	Res. Corps	Cav. Corps	Total	Wagons Auth.
Men (Officers + Enlisted present)-	26,160	13,894	16,129	18,747	7,593	82,523	
Inf. Regts.	57	37	40	40	NA	174x12	2,088
Cav. Regts.	NA	NA	NA	NA	19	19x25	475
Artillery Pieces	74	54	60	54	12	254x1	254
Brigades	12	9	9	9	5	44x5	220
Divisions	4	3	3	3	2	15x72	1,080
Div. Ord.						25x15	375
Div. Sup.						40x15	600
						TOTAL	**5,092**

Two explanations are possible as to why the number on hand was so much lower than the number authorized. First, the army could not acquire this many wagons because they were not available. But if this were the case, why would MG Rosecrans issue an order to limit the number of wagons when the limit he set was twice what could even be acquired. Also, why issue an order trying to reduce the number of wagons in the army and then make the authorization twice what is already on hand? A more reasonable explanation for the discrepancy is that the wagons listed do not include the ordnance and quartermaster wagons in the division trains. These wagons must have been considered, in modern military language, "off the books," controlled by the Ordnance and Quartermaster Departments so they did not have to be counted in the division and corps totals. The divisions were authorized to have 25 wagons in each division for an ammunition train and 40 per for supplies, for a total of 375 and 600, respectively, in the army. These trains must have been much larger than they were authorized on paper. There were also large army wide reserve trains: the ordnance train reported in Stevenson, Alabama by Assistant Secretary of War Dana in September numbered 800 wagons, that are unaccounted for in the authorizations or reports. There was probably an army reserve supply train also, though it has not been reported in the Official Records. So the inspection reports do not give a clear picture of how many wagons were with the army as it rolled out of its positions near Murfreesboro in late June. The total number with the army was closer to, and probably exceeded, the 5,092 authorized by MG Rosecrans and not the 2,411 on the inspection reports.[100]

This meant that if you used the 2,411 reported wagons with the 85,545 men present, you get 28 wagons per thousand men. If you use the 5,092 authorized wagons, you get 60 wagons per thousand. (Remember, Napoleon's ideal number was 12.5 per one thousand, LTG Grant would allow 19 per thousand and MG McClellan had 26 per thousand in his campaigns.) If, as will be seen in the next chapter, the corps did exceed their authorized number (as they were accused of doing), that meant they did have in excess of 5,092 wagons as they attempted to outmaneuver GEN Bragg's forces. This large number of wagons, and the excessive rains that ruined the unimproved roads, may very well have been the reason MG Rosecrans was not able to fight his decisive battle with GEN Bragg north of the Cumberland Plateau.

To conclude the analysis of the Union Army and the Army of the Cumberland's logistical system, a single commodity will be followed from the request for it in the field, back to the supplier, and forward again through the logistical channels. For example, a request for ammunition for a .58 caliber Springfield rifle coming from the 11th Michigan

Infantry of the 2d Brigade, 2d Division, XIV Army Corps in early June 1863 will be used. The regimental ordnance sergeant would compile his monthly report of the amount of ammunition on hand and the amount required and give this to the regimental quartermaster. This report would be passed to higher and compiled with other units at the brigade, division, and corps level by the senior ordnance officer in those units' headquarters.

At the Army level, CPT Porter would consolidate the reports. He could cross level ammunition between units or issue from the stocks on hand in Murfreesboro. If he could not fill the request, he would telegraph the ordnance depot in Nashville run by CPT Townsend. If he could not fill it, he sent it back to the regional ordnance depot in Louisville. If not filled there, the request went to the Ordnance Bureau in Washington.

They could fill the request from several places. The order could go to the largest facility for making rifle cartridges in the war, the Washington Arsenal (present day Fort NcNair.)[101] Here hundreds of women hand rolled the paper cartridges with 60 grains of powder (that could have come from the DuPont Powder Mills in Delaware) and a lead minié ball that was .5775 inches in diameter. Once rolled, the cartridge was packed in a wooden crate that held 1,000 rounds and 1,000 percussion caps.[102] The crate would be transported to the Baltimore & Ohio rail station near the foot of Capitol Hill where it would be loaded on a northbound train.[103]

The train would travel to Benwood, Virginia (south of Wheeling), on the Ohio River. There the crate would be unloaded from the car, ferried to Bellaire, Ohio, and loaded on a car of the Central Ohio Railroad and sent west to Columbus, then pass directly to the Indiana Central Railroad to Indianapolis. There the crate was unloaded and moved to the Jeffersonville, Madison, and Indianapolis Railroad for the trip south to Jeffersonville, Indiana on the Ohio River. There the crate would be unloaded, ferried across the Ohio and moved to the Ordnance Depot in Louisville to be received by the clerks. Once done, the crate would be loaded on a Louisville and Nashville railcar for the trip to Nashville.

In Nashville, the crate could either be unloaded and received by the ordnance clerks or the shipment could have been earmarked for throughput so the train would continue down the Nashville and Chattanooga Railroad to the Ordnance Depot in Fortress Rosecrans.[104] There the ordnance clerks would receive the crate and store it in their warehouse. The corps ordnance chief would be notified to pick up his cartridges and wagons would be sent to get the crate. Then the division wagons would pick up from the corps, the brigade from the division. The regimental ordnance sergeant would be sent to pick up the crate and once received, he would break down the crate and issue the cartridge to an 11th Michigan soldier.

This process was a mix of technological, administrative and military innovations that came together in the war and could not have been possible just 10 years prior. The men who created the system to feed, arm, clothe and move the Union armies were part of an amazing achievement that made victory possible.

---

[1]Christopher R. Gabel, *Railroad Generalship: Foundations of Civil War Strategy* (Combat Studies Institute, Command and General Staff College: Fort Leavenworth, Kansas, 1997), 1.

[2]Larry J. Daniel, *Days of Glory: the Army of the Cumberland, 1861-1865* (Baton Rouge, Louisiana: Louisiana State University Press, 2004), 181.

[3]Ibid., 183 ;and US War Department, *The War of the Rebellion: A Compilation of the Official Records of the Union and Confederate Armies*, Series I, vol. 23, part II, (Washington, DC: Government Printing Office, 1880-1901), 36 (hereafter cited as *OR*).

[4]Wiliam M. Lamers, *The Edge of Glory: A Biography of General William S. Rosecrans, U.S.A.* (Baton Rouge, Louisiana: Louisiana State University Press, 1999), 181-182.

[5]Ibid, 183, 244; and James Lee McDonough, *Stones River: Bloody Winter in Tennessee* (Knoxville, Tennessee: The University of Tennessee Press, 1980), 81, 216.

[6]Steven E. Woodworth, *Six Armies in Tennessee: The Chickamauga and Chattanooga Campaigns* (Lincoln, Nebraska: University of Nebraska Press, 1998), 10-12; Thomas L. Connelly, *Civil War Tennessee: Battles and Leaders* (Knoxville, Tennessee: The University of Tennessee Press, 1979), 10; McDonough, 28-29; George B. Davis, Leslie J. Perry, and Joseph W. Kirkley, *The Official Military Atlas of the Civil War* (Washington, DC: Government Printing Office, 1891), Plate XXIV, number 3; and Micheal R. Bradley, *Tullahoma: The 1863 Campaign for the Control of Middle Tennessee* (Shippensburg, Pennsylvania: Burd Street Press, 2000), 16.

[7]Connelly, 10; Davis, Plate XXIV; Woodworth, 143; Peter Cozzens, *The Battles for Chattanooga- National Parks Civil War Series* (Eastern National Park and Monument Association, 1996), 3; and Lenette S. Taylor, *The Supply for Tomorrow Must Not Fail: Civil War of Captain Simon Perkins Jr., a Union Quartermaster (*Kent, Ohio: The Kent State University Press, 2004.), 23, 50.

[8]Connelly, 10; Davis, Plate XXIV; and Taylor, 23, 76.

[9]James M. McPherson, *The Atlas of the Civil War* (New York: Macmillan, 1994), 46-47.

[10]Maury Klein, *History of the Louisville & Nashville Railroad* (Lexington, Kentucky: The University of Kentucky Press, 2003), 3-5.

[11]Ibid., 10.

[12]Ibid., 12, 17.

[13]Ibid., 13.

[14] Ibid., 23-24, 41.

[15]Ibid., 27-31.

[16]Erna Risch, *Quartermaster Support of the Army: A History of the Corps 1775-1939* (Washington, DC: Quartermaster Historian's Office, 1962), 396.

[17]Taylor, 124; Thomas Weber, *The Northern Railroads in the Civil War: 1861-1865* (Bloomington and Indianapolis, Indiana: Indiana University Press, 1952), 178, 187; and Risch, 401.

[18]Weber, 178.

[19]Ibid., 180, 188.

[20]George B. Abdill, *Civil War Railroads: A Pictorial Story of the War Between the States, 1861-1865* (Bloomington and Indianapolis, Indiana: Indiana University Press, 1961), 134.

[21]Klein, 31.

[22]Abdill, 132; Mark Zimmermann, *Guide to Civil War Nashville* (Nashville, Tennessee: Battle of Nashville Preservation Society, 2004), 25; and Davis, LXXIII.

[23]Taylor, 107-108.

[24]Richard E. Prince, *Nashville, Chattanooga & St. Louis Railway: History and Steam Locomotives* (Bloomington and Indianapolis, Indiana: Indiana University Press, 1967), 6; Woodworth, 143; Daniel, 109; Zimmermann, 10; and Flossie Carmicheal and Ronald Lee, *In and Around Bridgeport* (Collegedale, Tennessee: The College Press, 1967), 32-35, 37-39, 41-42.

[25]Prince, 7-10.

[26]Risch, 402.

[27]Davis, CII; Risch, 402; George H. Yater, *Two Hundred Years at the Falls of the Ohio: A History of Louisville and Jefferson County* (Louisville, Kentucky: The Heritage Corporation, 1979), 84-85; and Weber, 182.

[28]Weber, 180.

[29]*OR*, vol. 23, part II, 303.

[30]Taylor, 19, 67.

[31]Ibid., 85.

[32]Ibid., 74.

[33]Davis, Plates XXIV, CII, CIII.

[34]Taylor, 125-126; and Zimmermann, 24-25.

[35]Taylor, 122, 135, 141.

[36]Robert D. Richardson, "Rosecrans' Staff at Chickamauga: The Significance of Major General William S. Rosecrans' Staff on the Outcome of the Chickamauga Campaign" (master's thesis, US Army Command and General Staff College, Fort Leavenworth, Kansas:,1989), 190; and Taylor, 127.

[37]Taylor, 95; and Richardson, 32-33.

[38]Department of the Cumberland-Department of the Tennessee, *Monthly Inspection Reports Received (1863),* Record Group 393, vols. 239-243, National Archives, Washington, DC; Department of the Cumberland-Department of the Tennessee, *Consolidated Monthly Inspection Reports of Cavalry, XIV, XX, XXI, Army Corps (1863),* Record Group 393, E-1063, vol. 141, National Archives, Washington, DC and Department of the Cumberland-Department of the Tennessee, *Monthly Inspection Reports- Cavalry and Batteries (1863),* Record Group 393, vols. 239-243, National Archives, Washington, DC.

[39]Richardson, 31.

[40]Taylor, 108; and Bradley, 16-17.

[41]Richardson, 34.

[42]Taylor, 75; and Davis, 100-115.

[43]Micheal J. Davis, "The Role of Ordnance Logistics in the Chickamauga Campaign" (master's thesis, US Army Command and General Staff College, Fort Leavenworth, Kansas, 1995), 48.; Department of the Cumberland-Department of the Tennessee, *Monthly Inspection Reports Received (1863),* Record Group 393, vols. 239-243, National Archives, Washington, DC; and Department of the Cumberland-Department of the Tennessee, *Consolidated Monthly Inspection Reports of Cavalry, XIV, XX, XXI, Army Corps (1863),* Record Group 393, E-1063, vol. 141, National Archives, Washington, DC.

[44]Davis, 47, 100-115 ;and Monthly Inspection Reports 1863.

[45]Ibid., 58.

[46]Richardson, 36; and David A. Rubenstein, "A Study of the Medical Support to the Union and Confederate Armies During the Battle of Chickamauga: Lessons and Implications for Today's US Army Medical Department Leaders" (master's thesis, US Army Command and General Staff College, Fort Leavenworth, Kansas, 1990), 21-22.

[47]Ibid., 22 ;and *OR*, vol. 23, part II, 116.

[48]Rubenstein, 23.

[49]Taylor, 137-139.

[50]Rubenstein, 23-24; and Abdill, 120.

[51]Klein, 31.

[52]Taylor, 47-48.

[53]Klein, 30-33; and Taylor, 66-69, 78.

[54]Klein, 36.

[55]Ibid., 36.

[56]William L. Shea and Terrence J. Winschel, *Vicksburg is the Key: The Struggle for the Mississippi River* (Lincoln, Nebraska: University of Nebraska, 2003), 43-44.

[57]Zimmermann, 13.

[58]Ibid., 71;Stones River National Battlefield Informational Handout, *Stones River: Fortress Rosecrans,* National Park Service, U.S. Department of the Interior, 2000; Davis, Plate CXII; and *OR*, vol. 23, part II, 154.

[59]Taylor, 109.

[60]John Robertson, *Michigan in the War* (Lansing, Michigan: W.S. George and Co., State Printers and Binders, 1882), 494-498; and George H. Turner, *Record of Service of the First Michigan Engineers and Mechanics in the Civil War, 1861-1865* (Kalamazoo, Michigan: Ihling Bros. and Everard for Adjutant General's Office, 1903), viiii-xiii.

[61]Risch, 401.

[62]Daniel, 189; Lamers, 193; and *OR*, vol. 20, part I, 186.

[63]Woodworth, 4.

[64]*OR*, vol. 23, 7.

[65]Taylor, 109, 117.

[66]Woodworth, 4.

[67]Lamers, 187.

[68]Department of the Cumberland-Department of the Tennessee, *Monthly Inspection Reports- Cavalry and Batteries (1863),* Record Group 393, vols. 239-243, National Archives, Washington, DC; and Peter Cozzens, *This Terrible Sound* (Urbana and Chicago, Illinois: University of Illinois Press, 1992), 543-544.

[69]*OR*, vol. 23, part II, 33-34.

[70]Ibid., 22-23.

[71]Ibid., 31.

[72]Ibid., 34.

[73]Ibid., 37.

[74]Ibid., 174, 192, 199.

[75]Monthly Inspection Reports-Cavalry, April and May 1863.

[76]*OR*, vol. 23, part II, 245.

[77]Ibid., 246, 270.

[78]Ibid., 256.

[79]Ibid., 270

[80]Ibid., 271-272.

[81]Ibid., 274.

[82]Ibid., 281.

[83]Ibid., 288-289.

[84]Ibid., 300-304; and Taylor, 114-115.

[85]*OR*, vol. 23, part II, 320-321.

[86]Ibid., 336-337.

[87]Ibid., 351.

[88]Monthly Inspection Reports-Cavalry, May 1863

[89]Lamers, 275.

[90]Robert E. Harbison, "Wilder's Brigade in the Tullahoma and Chattanooga Campaigns of the American Civil War" (master's thesis, US Army Command and General Staff College, Fort Leavenworth, Kansas, 2002), 7, 17, 41.

[91]Harbison, 9, 18-19, 23.

[92]Woodworth, 24.

[93]*OR*, vol. 23, part II, 321.

[94]Ibid., 41.

[95]Ibid., 74.

[96]Ibid., 234.

[97]Ibid., 317.

[98]Ibid., 423.

[99] Ibid., 398.

[100]Department of the Cumberland-Department of the Tennessee, *Monthly Inspection Reports Received (1863),* Record Group 393, vols. 239-243, National Archives, Washington, D.C.; Department of the Cumberland-Department of the Tennessee, *Consolidated Monthly Inspection Reports of Cavalry, XIV, XX, XXI, Army Corps,* Record Group 393, E-1063, vol. 141, National Archives, Washington, D.C.; Cozzens, 537-544; Department of the Cumberland-Department of the Tennessee, *Monthly Inspection Reports--Cavalry and Batteries (1863).* Record Group 393, Vols. 239-243, National Archives, Washington, D.C. and *OR*, vol. 23, part II, 399.

[101]Richard M. Lee, *Mr. Lincoln's City: An Illustrated Guide to the Civil War Sites of Washington* (McLean, Virginia: EPM Publications, 1981), 154.

[102]Micheal J. Davis, "The Role of Ordnance Logistics in the Chickamauga Campaign" (master's thesis, US Army Command and General Staff College, Fort Leavenworth, Kansas, 1995), 20, 22.

[103]Lee, 39.

[104]Weber, 182.

CHAPTER 4

THE TULLAHOMA AND CHICKAMAUGA CAMPAIGNS: LOGISTICAL SUPPORT IN THE FIELD

> Logistics cannot be separated from tactics and strategy. It is a major factor in the execution of strategic and tactical conceptions, so inextricably interwoven that it is an integral part of each.[1]
>
> 1926 US Army Staff Text

GEN Bragg understood MG Rosecrans' difficult situation in 1863. To get to Chattanooga and free the Unionist people of east Tennessee, MG Rosecrans could not simply head east across the Cumberland Plateau. Even though crossing it would be difficult with the Army of the Cumberland having to haul all of its supplies in wagons through this region of little water and few farms to forage from, that was not the main challenge. The real problem MG Rosecrans faced if he took this course of action was how to refill his supply wagons once on the far side of the plateau in order to continue the campaign. Continuous wagon trains across the plateau would be slow, could not haul the required tonnage, and the forage for the mule teams would further limit the amount each wagon could carry. The valley of the Tennessee River, while fertile, was already supporting GEN Bragg's army and would be able to provide little for MG Rosecrans once he arrived there.

The Tennessee River was another option of invasion for MG Rosecrans. This would enable a supply line to reach back to the Ohio River and greatly ease the supply problems due to the greater amounts that a steamboat could carry than a rail car or wagon. As previously mentioned, the water levels dropped in the summer making the passage of the shoals and rapids on the river impossible. The only way that MG

Rosecrans could logistically sustain his army so far into this area of the South was by using the Nashville & Chattanooga Railroad (N&C). Because of this, following the Battle of Murfreesboro, GEN Bragg fell back to a new position north of Tullahoma, Tennessee with his corps running roughly west/ east from Shelbyville (Lieutenant General [LTG] Leonidas Polk's Corps) to Wartrace (LTG William Hardee's Corps) with forward forces of cavalry and infantry blocking the gaps through the Highland Rim. GEN Bragg sat in his headquarters in Tullahoma, squarely across the N&C, knowing that MG Rosecrans would have to come through him to continue south.[2]

MG Rosecrans felt he had to meet several conditions before he could move forward. He had finally expanded his cavalry force, augmented with mounted infantry, so it matched the Confederate forces in numbers and firepower; the railroad (and an efficient system for protecting and repairing it) was operational from Louisville to Murfreesboro; he could put in the field 20,000 more men than GEN Bragg (who had 47,000), and he had coordinated with MG Ambrose Burnside, who had replaced BG Wright as commander of the Department of the Ohio, to move through the Cumberland Gap toward Knoxville so they could protect each others flanks.

MG Burnside's move was to begin on 4 June but on 2 June MG Halleck abruptly shifted the IX Corps from MG Burnside's department to support MG Grant in the Vicksburg Campaign in Mississippi. So MG Burnside halted his movement. MG Halleck then told MG Rosecrans, in response to his refusal to move forward that, "If you can do nothing yourself, a portion of your troops must be sent to Grant's relief."[3] Then, after MG Rosecrans canvassed his division and corps commanders on the advisability of advancing, which 11 of 14 said "no" to doing, MG Halleck sent him a telegram on

16 June asking, "Is it your intention to move forward? A definite answer, yes or no, is required." MG Rosecrans understood this to mean move now or lose part of your command or even be relieved. He responded that he hoped to move by 21 June but it wasn't until 23 June that the army corps received their orders to advance. This was following confirmation that BG Morgan was heading north again with 2,300 troopers, thereby weakening the cavalry forces facing MG Rosecrans to around 10,000. (BG Forrest had been shot by one of his artillery officers on 13 June taking him out of the campaign.)[4]

The logistical issues that MG Rosecrans had used as his reasons for not advancing had been cleared up by the beginning of the traditional campaigning season, 1 May; still he failed to move. He was no longer hampered by logistics, as he had been in January, yet it took veiled threats from the War Department to compel him to use his army against GEN Bragg. This was to the detriment of MG Grant when GEN Bragg was able to send three divisions to GEN Joseph Johnson in Mississippi. Logistics was an enabler by May, BG James Garfield felt the army was ready to move in April, but it took MG Rosecrans until the third week in June to take advantage of it.[5]

The route he chose to advance on GEN Bragg had been discovered in May during the numerous foraging and scouting expeditions that MG Rosecrans sent out. What he discovered was that the area to his east was no longer controlled by Confederate cavalry and that the gaps in the Highland Rim to his south were also poorly covered by Confederate forces, as evidenced by COL Wilder being able to pass south through Liberty Gap and return north through Hoover's Gap.[6] The plan he developed was to send MGs Thomas, McCook, and Granger (supported by most of Stanley's cavalry) corps south through Hoover, Liberty, and Guy's Gaps, respectively, toward the Confederate corps dug in at Shelbyville and Wartrace. He sought to hold GEN Bragg's attention there so GEN Bragg could not react to MG Crittenden's corps, minus BG Van Cleve's Division garrisoning Fortress Rosecrans, moving to the east through Bradyville and south to Manchester. Once in Manchester, GEN Bragg's positions in Shelbyville and Wartrace would be flanked and he would have to retreat. The Union army would regroup in Manchester and at the same time try to capture and destroy the railroad bridge south of Tullahoma over the Duck River at Estill Springs to cut off GEN Bragg's retreat. If that was done, a decisive battle would be fought with GEN Bragg at a disadvantage and his army could be destroyed or captured before it could make it up the Cumberland Plateau.[7]

MG Rosecrans was figuring the Confederates would hold the gaps in the Highland Rim and then the fortifications north of Shelbyville and Wartrace for several days, allowing time for MG Crittenden to get behind them at Manchester. A quick moving cavalry brigade under COL H. G. Minty made it through Guy's Gap, COL T.J. Harrison's 39th Indiana Mounted Infantry pushed into Liberty Gap and COL Wilder's brigade stormed Hoover's Gap all on the first day of the campaign. By days end, infantry divisions had followed the mounted troops through and secured the gaps. The following days saw similar aggressive attacks by the Union army, which unnerved GEN Bragg and his corps commanders. COL Wilder was able to raid behind the Confederates and tear up N & C track at Decherd and cut the telegraph but could not destroy the bridge at Estill Springs because of an infantry division protecting it. With the raid on his communications, GEN Bragg and his commanders decided on a full retreat and started across the Cumberland Plateau. By 4 July, he had made a successful escape. MG

Rosecrans had cleared middle Tennessee of Confederates but he failed to bring them to a decisive engagement north of the Cumberland Plateau where he would have his greatest advantages.[8] The issues to be examined are what happened logistically to assist or hamper the Army of the Cumberland in the Tullahoma Campaign.

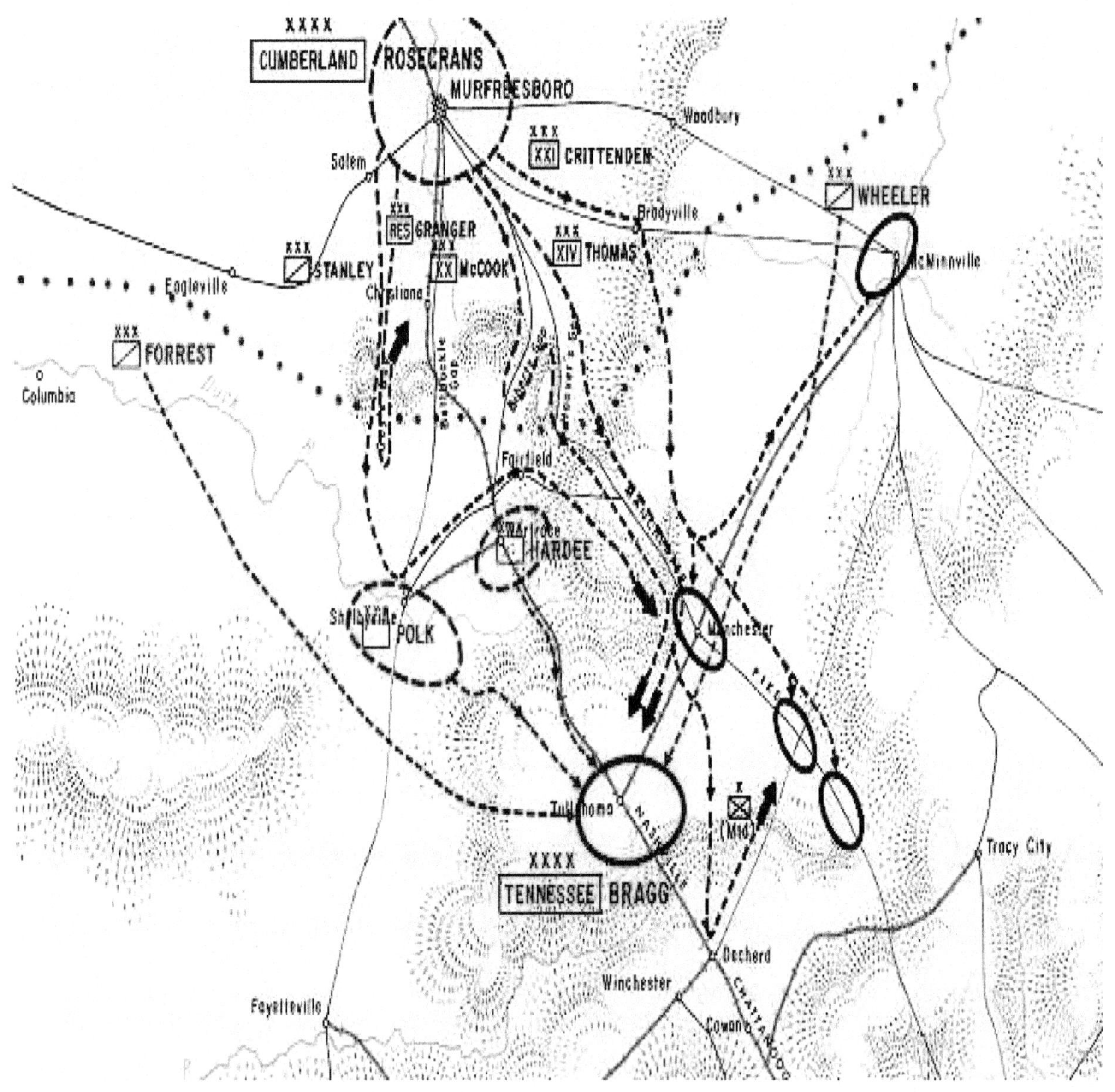

Figure 2. The Tullahoma Campaign

Source: www.nps.gov

Along with the 23 June orders detailing the corps routes for opening the campaign, each corps was given a separate order detailing logistical considerations. For example, here is the order given to MG Thomas:

> General: The general commanding directs you immediately to put your command in readiness for marching, with twelve days' rations. The rations will consist only of hard bread, coffee, sugar, and salt, and a half ration of pork. The remainder of the meat ration will be drawn on the hoof. You will prepare to move in light marching order, taking the smallest practicable amount of transportation and baggage. Put all your extra wagons into park on the north side of the Stone's River, under cover of the works, and send all your extra baggage to the fortification for safe-keeping.[9]

MG Rosecrans did not specify a change to the number of wagons authorized from what he had allowed the previous winter. It is obvious he expected the corps to reduce the number of wagons in their regiments and trains to increase their marching speed. He sought to maneuver GEN Bragg from his fortifications and fight him on ground of his own choosing before GEN Bragg could properly react to his movements. This could only happen with a quick, agile force that was not slowed by lengthy wagon trains. The corps commanders passed the order down to their division commanders but the compliance by the divisions was mixed and had consequences on the outcome of the campaign.

On 24 June it began to rain. This rain lasted for 17 days and turned the roads of middle Tennessee into a quagmire. MG Rosecrans described the wet soil as being, "so soft and spongy that wagons cut into it as if it as if it were a swamp, and even horses cannot pass over it without similar results."[10] This situation, coupled with the excessive number of wagons, ruined the roads as a marching surface. MG Crittenden's corps was meant to be the swift maneuver wing of the army but the mud in the Barrens slowed him to a crawl. Mules and horses floundered in the roads in mud up to their noses. Teams were unhitched and up to 50 men at a time lifted and pulled the wagons with ropes. It would take from the 24th to the 27th of June for MG John Palmer's infantry division and BG John Turchin's cavalry brigade to move their units to the summit of the Highland Rim, just 21 miles. BG Thomas Wood's division followed once they cleared the road, and he made it in just 11 hours.[11] He had this to say about wagons in his after action report:

> The commanding general of the Army of the Cumberland issued the order of preparation for an immediate advance on the 23d ultimo. This order required the troops to move as light as possible, taking with them twelve days' subsistence for the men and six days' forage for the animals, and leaving behind all unnecessary baggage. Three days' [supply] of the subsistence were ordered to be carried by the men in haversacks; the remainder of the rations, less six days' [supply] of meat to be driven, to be transported on wheels, allowing the smallest amount of baggage for the comfort and convenience of officers, the smallest limit of cooking utensils for the men and officers, and including twelve days' subsistence for the officers. I directed my staff officers to make an accurate and close computation, with a view to determining the least number of wagons that would move the division, taking with it all that it was required to transport by the preparatory order. The computation showed that six wagons per regiment for the weaker regiments and seven for the stronger regiments would fulfill the conditions of the problem. The preparations were all concluded during the afternoon and early evening of the 23d. . . . The neglect of other commanders in this army to conform to this order of preparation and the consequent embarrassment of the movements on the march, and the retardation of the concentration at Manchester, caused by the immense and overloaded baggage trains which they took with them . . . if it had been a free road, not cut up by heavy trains, and unimpeded by troops in front of it, it [his division] could have reached Manchester by nightfall Friday, the 26th.[12]

MG Palmer in his report says he received the preparatory order at 1500 hours on the 23d and had to spend the evening of the 23d and early morning of the 24th receiving rations from Murfreesboro (12 miles away) and issuing them out. Because of this, he did not have time to reduce his number of wagons and have them sent to Fortress Rosecrans like BG Wood had done.[13] But BG William Hazen, one of MG Palmer's brigade commanders, stated that he planned on reducing his baggage to seven wagons per regiment and two for brigade headquarters, but received an order at 0500 hours on the

24th from division to move with all his wagons. He sent a messenger to division that verified the order.[14] So the division commander made the call to move with all of his wagons instead of reducing the wagons in the evening and sending the excess ones to Fortress Rosecrans as he moved out towards Bradyville. MG Palmer could not have known the consequences of his actions which, coupled with the tremendous rainfall and clay and sand roads, slowed a possible three day march to a six day march. The lack of supervision by MG Crittenden to ensure the command was ready to perform its role with the speed required was a great failure on his part and helped GEN Bragg's army escape without a decisive battle being fought.

MG Crittenden's corps was not the only unit having difficulty moving swiftly on the roads on middle Tennessee. When MG Thomas was able to break through Hoover's Gap on 24 June, MG Rosecrans encouraged him to drive onto Manchester. MG McCook was recalled from Liberty Gap on the 26th to follow MG Thomas through Hoover's Gap. The problem was MG Thomas' wagon train had also not been reduced like MG Rosecrans had desired; his division commanders do not mention in their reports receiving such an order. MG Thomas does not mention any issue of slowed movement and only one division commander, MG James Negley, third in the line of march mentions, "My march was rendered very slow and difficult in consequence of the roughness of the road, which was very badly cut up by the trains in advance. . . . Found the road blocked with the trains of Generals Reynolds and Rousseau."[15] While the XIV Corps does not describe being greatly delayed by the wagons on the wet roads (they made it to Manchester on the morning of the 27th), MG McCook and his corps found the roads very difficult to traverse.

MG McCook also failed to mention any reduction in his wagon trains in his report of the campaign. BG Richard Johnson said his division received orders to draw the 12 days rations and six days forage but did not say he was ordered to reduce his wagon train.[16] MG Philip Sheridan, whose division led the XX Corps to Hoover's Gap on 26 June, said, "My march was so impeded by wagon trains in my front that my whole division did not reach Hoover's Gap till the morning of the 27th."[17] It took him a full day to march approximately seven miles. What MG Sheridan was running into was the large wagon trains of the XIV Corps, along with elements of the Pioneer Brigade hauling the pontoon trains in preparation for bridging the rain swollen Duck and Elk Rivers. MG McCook mentioned, "The road being bad, and blocked by General Morton's pontoon train," when attempting to get his divisions to Manchester.[18] BG Morton says his brigade broke camp at the entrance to Hoover's Gap at 0500 hours on 27 June and started south. "The roads being heavy and blocked up in various places with the transportation of the different corps, we made but slow progress with our pontoon train."[19] The poor planning by MG Rosecrans now had two army corps moving on the Manchester Pike with dozens of wooden pontoons sandwiched between them along with hundreds of wagons and artillery pieces.

The crowded road, large wagon trains, poor marching timetables, and incessant rains worked to delay the swift movements hoped for by MG Rosecrans. In frustration he issued another directive on 28 June to all his corps commanders;

> The general commanding has noticed with great regret the criminal neglect to obey department orders in reference to the reduction of baggage. If this army fails in the great object of the present movement, it will be mainly due to the fact that our wagons have been loaded down with unauthorized baggage. . . . The general commanding directs that all baggage trains be reduced to the minimum.

> To effect this, all tents, except shelter tents and one wall tent to each regiment, will be dispensed with. The ammunition now carried in the company wagons will be turned over to the division ordnance officers, who will be furnished with a sufficient number of additional wagons to transport it. This will enable the transportation of each regiment to be reduced to seven wagons, which the reduction will be made at once. All wagons in excess to this allowance will be turned over to the division quartermaster, who will, under the direction of the chief quartermaster of each corps, organize them into supply trains for the division...[20]

The corps apparently did not comply with this new order. None of the reports mention reducing their wagon trains and sending excess wagons back to Murfreesboro. LTC James Kerr of the 74th Illinois Infantry, escorted wagons of all three division of the XX Corps back to Murfreesboro from 30 June to 2 July. He mentioned finding a great deal of equipment and army property having been dumped on the sides of the roads by teamsters and soldiers trying to lightened their loads to get through the mud, but he did not mention turning in wagons to the quartermaster at Murfreesboro. Most likely, he was getting a new issue of forage since the six days of supply would have already been used up. He had the wagons back with the divisions in Tullahoma on 8 July.[21]

On 22 July, another General Order was issued stating that each regiment could have one wagon for the field officers and staff, one wagon for the medical department, one for the quartermaster's department, and one for every 75 company officers and men. The rest would be organized into trains at the division level.[22]

The orders do say to cut the number of wagons in the regiments, but they seem to allow these cut wagons to be gathered in the division ordnance and quartermaster trains and not sent back to Fortress Rosecrans. By looking at the numbers of wagons listed in the numbered corps inspection reports from May and July there is a reduction in wagons:

	XIV	XX	XXI Corps	
May	1,056	548	479	Total- 2,083
July	725	375	470	Total- 1,570

It does seem that MG Rosecrans' directive was complied with at least after the campaign ended on 5 July. But was there really a reduction of wagons or, as discussed earlier, did these wagons just get shifted off of the corps' books and get assigned to the ordnance and quartermaster department books yet still follow the same divisions as before? This seems possible, and likely, given the record of the units as discussed in the previous chapter.

Where does the fault lie in this fiasco? The corps had been given very specific authorizations during the winter for wagons. MG Rosecrans never issued additional instruction to reduce the number of wagons until 23 June, the day before they were to begin the campaign, when he told the corps commanders, "You will prepare to move in light marching order, taking the smallest practicable amount of transportation and baggage." This is a vague order leaving it up to the corps commanders to decide what they needed to take when they moved out. None of them could have foreseen the intense rain and its effect on the roads. Their decisions not to uniformly enforce across their commands a reduction in wagons and baggage had a serious impact on the course of the campaign and ensured a future battle would be fought with the Army of Tennessee south of the Cumberland Plateau, with the Army of the Cumberland at a severe disadvantage. In the end, the fault lay with MG Rosecrans and his last minute change and vague orders.

Dr. Perin, the army's Medical Director, showed in his report of the campaign that the army was well prepared medically to fight a large battle. The hospitals in Murfreesboro sent their patients to Nashville to free up bed space and additional buildings were prepared to receive the expected large number of casualties. 250 hospital tents were carried with the army's field hospitals and each regiment had its full compliment of medical supplies as well as reserve supplies carried with each corps. Each day of the campaign the wounded that were gathered up in the division hospitals were transported back to Murfreesboro so as not to encumber the army. The relatively few casualties for the campaign were unexpected; Dr. Perin lists 84 dead, 473 wounded, and 13 captured or missing for the army during the campaign. He cites the organization of the brigade ambulance trains for special recognition for their performance.[23]

No reports are available in the Official Records for the Quartermaster, Commissary or Ordnance Departments for the Tullahoma Campaign. Due to the short duration, amount of supplies with the corps, minimal fighting, and proximity to the railhead and depot at Fortress Rosecrans, few issues must have come up in these areas warranting a report from the officers in charge.

By 4 July, the Army of the Cumberland was at the foot of the Cumberland Plateau near Cowan, Tennessee. The large battle that was expected had not happened and MG Rosecrans found his pursuit stifled because of the problem of logistics. The railroad south of Murfreesboro was in terrible condition and unable to push the supplies to him that he required. He needed to stop and rebuild it before he could move on. Problems arose during the period between the end of the Tullahoma Campaign (4 July) and the crossing of the Tennessee River starting the Chickamauga Campaign (29 August) because MG Rosecrans and his staff failed to create a comprehensive logistical plan for the next phase of the campaign for Chattanooga.

Critical to the next phase of the operation was the 1st Michigan Engineers & Mechanics and the Pioneer Brigade and their work on the roads and railroads. Each numbered army corps had four companies of Pioneers attached to it for Tullahoma. The remainder of the brigade moved on 25 June behind MG Thomas, causing some of the traffic jam on the Manchester Pike. In BG Morton's report, he stated they were active in corduroying roads (cutting down trees and laying logs across the roads to stop the wagons from sinking in the mud), repairing wagon bridges over creeks and rivers, reconstructing depot buildings, and cutting firewood for locomotives. (BG Morton would resign in August citing poor health but probably also stung by the criticism he received for his unit's poor discipline and clogging of the road during Tullahoma. He returned to the army as the chief engineer on 17 September but did not resume as the commander of the Pioneer Brigade.)[24]

The 1st Michigan Engineers & Mechanics stayed in its camps around Murfreesboro until ordered to repair and open the railroad; they started their task on 29 June. COL Innes found that two and a half miles of iron had been pulled up from the rail bed between Bellbuckle and Wartrace. COL Anderson, Department Superintendent of Railroads, was ordered to have new rails brought in and put in place. The 1st Michigan then rebuilt the 350 foot bridge over the Duck River, a 150 foot bridge at Normandy, and, most impressively, the 60-foot high, 450-foot long Elk River bridge in 8 eight days, with the cooperation of the Pioneer Brigade. Their efforts enabled the railroad to be operational across the Elk River by 13 July.[25]

Next these two units had to repair the railroad south to Cowan, then through the tunnel under the Cumberland Plateau (which the Confederates failed to destroy, possibly closing the railroad for months) to Stevenson and then Bridgeport, Alabama on the Tennessee River. They had this completed by 25 July under the supervision of MG Philip Sheridan's division, with two of his brigades at Bridgeport and one at Stevenson.[26]

Within three weeks of the close of the Tullahoma Campaign, the railroad was open to the Tennessee River, yet MG Rosecrans failed to move. He felt the logistical base at Stevenson that he was building was not sufficient; he decided he must also have one at Tracy City. Tracy City sat on the top of the Cumberland Plateau in a coal region. The railroad spur that ran to it was built to haul coal down to the mainline and was built on such a step grade it needed a special locomotive to pull cars on it. For whatever reason, MG Rosecrans decided nothing could go forward until this depot was ready at Tracy City, an isolated site that would play a small role in the campaign. Things were held up because the special locomotive was damaged and a replacement that was found was also damaged while being shifted south from Nashville. It could not be repaired until 12 August. MG Rosecrans stated in his report for the Chickamauga Campaign, "It was deemed best, therefore, to delay the movement of the troops until that road was completely available for transporting stores to Tracy City." MG Rosecrans saw Tracy City as the best place to resupply units advancing on Chattanooga north of the river (to be discussed later), but he allowed the lack of a single locomotive to hold up the movement of the entire army for 17 days.[27]

With the railroad operational, the next logistical hurdle to overcome was the lack of rail cars to haul the proper tonnage the army needed. The region the Army of the Cumberland was now operating in had limited food and forage. The Tennessee River was not an option for resupply even though the rains had kept it and the Cumberland River navigable until the end of July; water levels were too unpredictable and it was unsafe with Confederates controlling the south side of the river.[28] The Nashville & Chattanooga railroad had to be used.

Even though the Louisville & Nashville listed 43 locomotives, 364 freight cars and 43 passenger cars on its books for 1863, the Army of the Cumberland was not able to get enough of its freight hauled to Nashville and beyond.[29] The problem was the lack of cars available to MG Rosecrans from this private corporation. Most of the rolling stock of the Nashville & Chattanooga railroad had been taken south by the Confederates and what was not taken was in poor condition. The Louisville & Nashville railroad now had to furnish cars to cover its line and assist the N&C. There were not enough cars available to the quartermasters to meet the needs of the army. The Chief Quartermaster, LTC Taylor sent the following compilation of cars required per day for supplying the army on 8 August. (He had submitted his resignation on 27 July citing health reasons. CPT Henry Hodges was promoted to LTC and made Chief Quartermaster.) (see table 5):

Table 5. Railcars Required

	Animals	Men	Pounds	Tons	No. of Cars
Forage	45,000		450,000	225	28
Rations		70,000	2,110,000	105	13
QM Stores			160,000	80	10
Med. Stores			32,000	16	2
Contingencies			112,000	56	7
Total Per Day-			**2,864,000 lbs**	**482 tons**	**60 cars**

Source: OR, vol. 23, part II, 601.

CPT Simon Perkins, the quartermaster in Nashville who was responsible for shipping goods south by rail, could not find the cars he needed. The 60 carloads LTC Taylor listed also enabled a gradual buildup of supplies in Stevenson for the future offensive campaign; MG Rosecrans wanted 20 days of supply on hand.[30] CPT Perkins needed to send 41 carloads so the army could survive each day, which was difficult. Once CPT Perkins sent the cars south, there was no telling when he would get them back. Some days he only had 11 cars to send and on 10 July he could send no commissary stores at all.[31] To alleviate this problem, MG Rosecrans purchased 50 freight cars for the railroad and began commandeering express cars to haul government freight. By 9 August, two trains a day were arriving in Bridgeport, enabling troops and animals along the entire line to receive adequate food and forage and continue building up the stockpile in Stevenson, but the issue of railcars was not settled. [32] The problems with the arrangements between the L&N and the Army were becoming obvious back in Washington and prompted BG Meigs to telegraph COL Swords that, "The management of the railroads in the west, so far as they are under military control, is little understood here." The political influence of L&N President Guthrie kept his line in private hands and this peculiar relationship between it and the government going throughout the war.[33]

On 10 August, COL Anderson resigned from his position as Superintendent of Railroads, probably due to the criticism he received from MG Rosecrans. MG Rosecrans made COL Innes "dual hatted" as the new Superintendent while he remained commander of the 1st Michigan Engineers & Mechanics. He continued in this position until after MG Rosecrans' relief in October and COL Anderson was reinstated.[34]

The month-long problem with the railroads was inexcusable. Many of the individual parts of the team needed to run the line, the engineers and the quartermasters, worked extremely well and did great service in putting the line in working order and pushing cars to the troops. The overall planning, however, needed to run the line once the army occupied the region was non-existent. MG Rosecrans was in Murfreesboro for six months planning his move south. Even though he thought a major decisive battle would be fought north of the Cumberland Plateau and, therefore, resupply from Murfreesboro would not be a concern, he needed to plan ahead for his pursuit of the enemy and the occupation of Chattanooga. He failed to understand what he needed to operate a railroad to the Tennessee River, let alone into Chattanooga and north Georgia. Why the number of rail cars and locomotives he needed were not ready for use in Nashville once he took over the N&C is inexcusable. He failed to give COL Anderson, and possibly LTC Taylor, proper direction to plan ahead for this issue. It cost him many weeks to overcome the oversight.

After several weeks of exchanged letters and telegrams with MG Halleck, all attempting to prod MG Rosecrans into offensive movement, MG Rosecrans finally moved his army over the Cumberland Plateau on 16 August and his headquarters to Stevenson on 18 August. There the preparations for crossing the Tennessee River and future logistical support were finalized.[35]

Stevenson became the forward logistical hub for the army south of the Cumberland Plateau due to its location. The town site was selected because the valley formed by the Big Crow Creek begins there and cuts north through the Plateau. The valley ended before the entire Plateau was breached but it required just the 2,228 foot tunnel to cut through to Cowan, Tennessee on the far side. The N&C would lay its tracks down the Big Crow Creek Valley and where they turned and headed east, the Memphis and Charleston Railroad joined them. This juncture became the town of Stevenson.[36]

When the site was occupied the previous summer, numerous fortifications were begun to protect the supply depot that was built. In all, seven blockhouses, two unfinished redoubts, and two forts were built to encircle the town. The largest fort was Fort Harker, a 150-foot square, 14-foot high earthwork with an eight-foot dry moat and seven cannon platforms. The fort was built on high ground north of town and fire from its guns would have swept the approaches to the supply depot.[37]

The town itself was small, consisting of a few dozen homes and a row of buildings fronting the train depots' that served as the business district. The largest hotel, the Alabama House, was located here. The small brick house that served as MG Rosecrans' headquarters was approximately ½ mile east of the depot.[38] The depot had to be greatly expanded to store the supplies needed by tens of thousands of men and thousands of horses and mules. Warehouses and storage platforms all had to be built at the site and half of the field hospital at Murfreesboro (750 beds) was transferred down, (the other half was in Cowan.)[39]

Ten miles east of Stevenson was Bridgeport, the site where the railroad crossed the Tennessee River. The Confederates had understood the importance of the railroad bridge and started defensive works on a hill overlooking the west end of the bridge in 1862. BG Mitchell's occupying Union troops continued to improve the works and the site was called Battery or Fort Hill. These same works were occupied by BG William H. Lytle's brigade of MG Sheridan's Division in July 1863. The site did not have a large supply depot during the Chickamauga Campaign, but in the weeks following the battle, it became a major logistical hub as the link via steamboats between the end of the rail line and the Army of the Cumberland in Chattanooga.[40]

The bridge consisted of two parts, the western 1,232-foot span to Long Island in the middle of the river and the eastern 428-foot span. The eastern span was the critical one; it contained a draw bridge that would open to allow steamboats to pass through the main shipping channel. Since it had more intricate parts and engineering, it would be more difficult to repair or replace. The entire length of the bridge was double decked. The top deck carried the trains over and the bottom deck was planked for wagon travel. When the Confederates evacuated Bridgeport in July, they destroyed six of the nine sections of the western span but did not injure the more critical eastern span. GEN Bragg also had burned the 780-foot railroad bridge over the 116-foot deep ravine of Running Water Creek near Whiteside, Tennessee, a site that lies between Sand Mountain and Raccoon Mountain.[41] With these bridges down and no steamers available, MG Rosecrans could not rely on resupply by rail once he crossed the Tennessee River; everything he needed would have to be hauled in wagons over and around the Sand and Lookout Mountain ranges that lay east of Bridgeport and south of Chattanooga. This question of resupply was as important to the future campaign as the location and disposition of the enemy. Without food, forage, and ammunition resupply capabilities, a campaign on the far side of the mountains was doomed to failure. President Lincoln had telegraphed on 1 August, "I rather think that by great exertions you can get to East Tennessee; but a very important question is, can you stay there."[42]

Without the ability to resupply his army on the far side of the mountains, MG Rosecrans would only be able to fight one large-scale battle. If he won that battle, he would not have the supplies readily available to his army to follow up his victory. The 26 miles of unusable rail line between Bridgeport and Chattanooga, and the lack of steamboats as a substitute, was an enormous problem for the Army of the Cumberland. Strangely, the general that had spent such a large amount of time making logistical preparations in Murfreesboro and Tullahoma disregarded these issues, issues that were much greater than any logistical problem he had yet faced, and plunged across the mountain in pursuit of the retreating Confederates.[43]

On 16 August the corps moved out. MG Crittenden's corps, supported by COL Minty's cavalry brigade and COL Wilder's mounted infantry brigade, moved east from Pelham, Manchester and McMinnville across the Cumberland Plateau into the valley of the Sequatchaie River Valley. MG Thomas' units moved south from Cowan and University and were strung out along the Tennessee River from Battle Creek, north of Bridgeport, to Stevenson. The remaining divisions of MG McCook's Corps moved to Stevenson and south to Bellefonte. The remaining three brigades of MG Stanley's cavalry were strung out between Bridgeport in the east to Huntsville and Decatur, Alabama in the west to watch the western flank.[44]

Wilder's brigade, followed closely by MG Crittenden's corps, crossed over the Cumberland Plateau, through the Sequatchie Valley and up Walden's Ridge which he descended to reach the river bank across from Chattanooga on 21 August. He began an infrequent shelling of the city, throwing the surprised Confederates into "consternation" and accelerating their evacuation of the city and its military stores and equipment south along the Western & Atlantic Railroad toward Atlanta. By that date, all of the Army of the Cumberland was poised along the Tennessee River.[45]

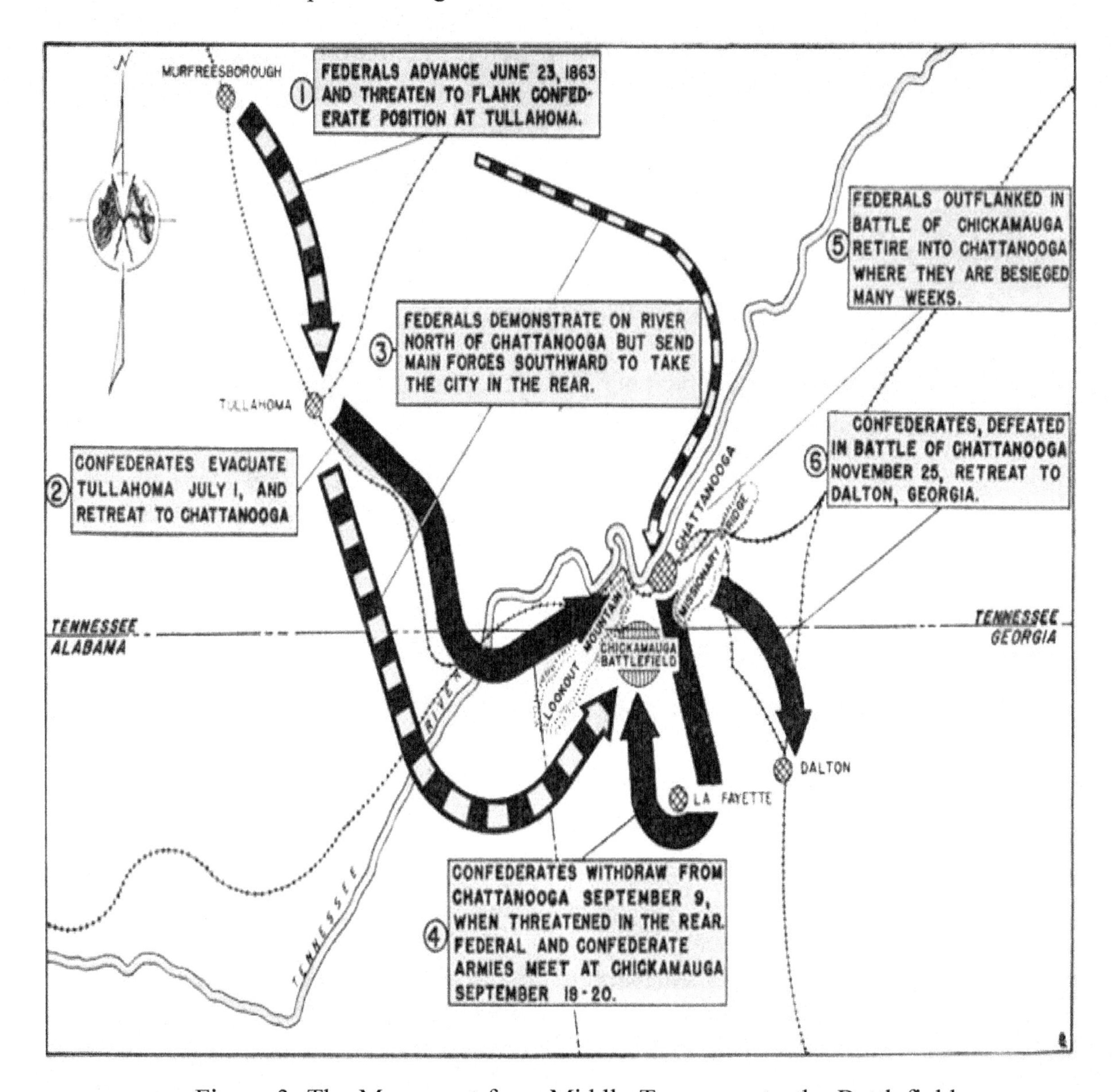

Figure 3. The Movement from Middle Tennessee to the Battlefield
Source: www.nps.gov

Since the railroad was open to Stevenson and Bridgeport, the units stationed there could easily draw supplies. The XXI Corps was supposed to be able to draw supplies from the depot so painstakingly set up at Tracy City. The problem was that Tracy City was not stocked with supplies when the movement began. As MG Crittenden's men approached the Tennessee River after five days of marching, they were in need of resupply, especially forage. Empty wagon convoys were sent to Tracy City but no supplies were found.[46] The division at the north end of the Sequatchie Valley at Pikeville was able to send trains across to the railhead at McMinnville for supplies. The units at the south end of the valley were also forced to send their wagons approximately 60 road miles to McMinnville instead of 30 road miles to Tracy City. Since McMinnville was not intended as the supply point for an entire corps, it quickly ran out of supplies to issue. The problem still had not been satisfactorily fixed on 24 August when MG Crittenden asked for and received permission to draw supplies from Bridgeport-Stevenson to fill his now empty wagons.[47]

In Stevenson, the issues were forwarding pontoons, lumber and, yet again, railcars. The pontoons are first mentioned in a dispatch on 12 August by MG Rosecrans as priority to go forward to Stevenson as soon as enough forage arrives.[48] On 17 August he told COL Innes to get the men to load the pontoons and the pontoons ready to be sent.[49] On 18 Aug, Lieutenant George Burroughs, a staff engineer, gave this status of the pontoon locations:

> The pontoons formerly at Manchester are now at Elk River Bridge. 30 at Elk River Bridge, 10 at Murfreesboro, 64 at Nashville. Wagons for 30 pontoons are with Pioneer Brigade. The other wagons at Nashville, being supplied with mules, etc. Railroad men telegraph me that they have 7 flats, which they want to load with supplies if they are not needed at once for pontoons. . . . When do you want the pontoons shipped?[50]

Why these 104 pontoons were still scattered all the way back to Nashville while the army was sitting at the rivers edge, why the wagons to haul the pontoons still did not all have properly equipped mule teams and why these teams were scattered back to Nashville is not explained and is certainly a gross oversight in planning. The pontoons, minus the wagons, did arrived six miles from Stevenson on 20 August and MG Negley was assigned the task of downloading them from the flatcars in the Big Crow Creek Valley and concealing them from Confederate view. [51] The number of pontoons was also inadequate. MG Rosecrans certainly understood that more than one bridge would be necessary as crossing sites for his army and the supply trains that would be moving back and fourth, yet there were enough pontoons for only a single crossing site available in mid-August. Why more were not purchased or built during the six months at Murfreesboro or during the six week stay around Tullahoma is unexplained but it was another terrible oversight. The pontoons should have been pre-positioned at Cowan ready to immediately follow the army across the plateau and there should have been enough pontoons for at least two, preferably three, crossing sites available. MG Rosecrans did order LTC Kinsman A. Hunton, of the 1st Michigan Engineers and Mechanics, to build 50 pontoons after the Bridgeport bridge was completed on 2 September. These new pontoons were completed on 10 September by a battalion of the 1st Michigan.[52]

Since there were not going to be enough pontoons for two bridges, and Caperton's Ferry southeast of Stevenson was where the pontoon bridge went in, MG Sheridan, BG Lytle and LTC Hunton, made plans to build a bridge at Bridgeport. They began requesting lumber from Nashville for flooring and sent 1,500 soldiers into nearby woods to cut 1,500 logs to build an "A" frame trestle bridge. Since they could not get enough wood from Nashville, the local houses, business, and barns were stripped of their siding to provide flooring. MG Sheridan later remembered just four or five pontoons being available for the "swimming deep" parts of the channels, though engineer LT George Burroughs wrote in a 1 September telegram that "26 barges" helped make up the bridge. No other mention of the barges is made though some shallow boats can be clearly seen in the photographs of the bridge taken at this time.[53]

Too few railcars and locomotives to haul supplies was still an issue. On 15 August, MG Rosecrans telegraphed the Adjutant General, BG Lorenzo Thomas, in Washington that, "Movement of my main force was delayed a week by want of cars."[54] Eighty rail cars were contracted for purchase (20 from the Adams Express Company) by 20 August, as well as "a number" of cars being located at Michigan City, Indiana and Cumberland City, Tennessee and directed toward the Department of the Cumberland.[55] MG Rosecrans received confirmation from CPT Charles Parsons, a quartermaster in St. Louis, on 26 August that 50 boxcars that he requested were being shipped to him.[56] On 2 September, CPT Parsons telegraphed that he was trying to send the cars by river to Louisville, but could not get transportation for them.[57] On 7 September, MG Rosecrans, in an attempt to get more railcars made available, telegraphed President Guthrie of the L&N that he must have 20 cars daily just for the commissary stores along with whatever cars the quartermaster required.[58] On the 9th, Mr. Guthrie responded that the delay with the cars was not with the L&N but with the slow unloading of cars in Nashville.[59] CPT William Russell, a quartermaster in Nashville, wrote MG Gordon Granger, commander of the region north of the Cumberland Plateau, on 9 September that:

> The number of cars furnished by the Louisville and Nashville Railroad for transportation of Government freight will average about 21 cars per day, of which 9 to 12 have been filled with commissary stores. This is exclusive of cattle which are shipped by the conductors. It will require at least 20 cars per day for commissary stores alone. This will feed the army, but leave no surplus. There

> should be at least 60 cars per day for transportation of government stores. The Nashville and Chattanooga, with a limited amount of rolling stock, furnishes 65 cars per day.[60]

CPT Parsons also telegraphed MG Grant in Mississippi to ask him for locomotives. MG Hurlbut telegraphed from Memphis to MG Rosecrans on 11 September that, "Six locomotives can be spared for your use from this place."[61] Whether these locomotives arrived before Chickamauga is not mentioned.

Since LTC Taylor had sent his report on the number of railcars needed each day to MG Rosecrans on 8 August, the shortage of railcars must have been known since then and probably well before. Why the railcar shortage was not properly anticipated by COL Anderson and LTC Hodges during the winter, and plans put in place to fix it, is not explained. An assumption could have been that the L&N would augment them more than they did on the N&C. Any augmentation or sharing of L&N cars on the N&C must have been minimal; most of the freight seems to have been shipped to Nashville and unloaded from L&N cars and reloaded on N&C cars. How much of this MG Rosecrans knew about is not known but the system as it existed was unworkable. Surging supplies when needed was not possible with Mr. Guthrie being allowed to manage his line purely as a money making venture as opposed to a vital part of the logistics chain for the Army of the Cumberland. The inability or unwillingness of MG Rosecrans, or the government in Washington, to force Mr. Guthrie to comply with the number of cars needed to supply the army was putting the army, on the verge of a dangerous undertaking, at even greater risk.

Rebuilding the permanent bridges needed at Bridgeport and Running Water were going to be bigger undertakings than the engineers with the army could handle during active campaigning. The situation was made worse on 14 August when Confederates burned the eastern span of the Bridgeport bridge that contained the draw bridge.[62] To rebuild this bridge the McCollum Bridge Company out of Cincinnati was contracted by LTC Hodges. A "Mr. Boomer" was the contractor of the Running Water Bridge.[63] Mr. Guthrie was informed of these new projects on 2 September and instructed to haul any materiel they might need to bring to the sites.[64] These structures were not completed until January 1864, four months after the Chickamauga Campaign.[65] The Confederates were certainly aided in their ability to burn this bridge by the slow moving Union army. With too few railcars to push supplies rapidly forward and no pontoons in place with which the Union forces could make a quick attack across the river, the Confederates had several weeks to watch BG Lytle's brigade in Bridgeport before they decided to burn the eastern span. Better anticipation of logistical needs and having the proper logistical support in place in July would have enabled this span to be saved and the repair of the line to Chattanooga would have happened weeks, if not months, earlier.

Part of the problem with understanding what was happening on the ground was that many of the officers responsible for the logistics of the army were back in Nashville. LTC Simmons, the Chief of Commissary, and COL Innes, the Superintendent of Railroads were there and LTC Hodges, the Chief Quartermaster, did not arrive in Stevenson until 19 August after a 20 day leave in New York. CPT Porter, Chief of Ordnance, and Dr. Perin, the Medical Director, moved down to Stevenson and apparently crossed the river with the army commander.[66] This, the officers' dual roles as Department and Army of the Cumberland staff officers, and the personnel changes in the Superintendent of Railroads, Chief Quartermaster, and Chief Engineer positions during the month prior to the move across the river, may explain some of the planning problems the army faced.

MG Rosecrans was also distracted from his main effort of capturing Chattanooga, to free east Tennessee and cut the rail link with Virginia, by secondary concerns. He contacted Military Governor Andrew Johnson on 27 August that he was trusting to him the building of the Nashville & Northwestern Railroad, a link between Nashville and Johnsonville, a town west of Nashville on the Tennessee River. This was apparently meant to be an alternate supply route to the N&C and the Cumberland River. The line was constructed in 1863-64. But the timing of the construction was bad. If it was to be built it should have been during the winter and spring before the campaigning began. By beginning it in August, MG Rosecrans was diverting limited railroad materiel, guards and labor from MG Granger's security forces, and two valuable companies from the 1st Michigan Engineers and Mechanics to build from scratch a new rail line that would not be ready for many months. These resources would have been better used repairing the rail line between Bridgeport and Chattanooga or building steamboats to move supplies forward to the army in Chattanooga, a dire and immediate need.[67]

MG Rosecrans also had dispatched MG Lovell H. Rousseau to Washington to lobby Secretary Stanton for the resources to mount his infantry division and arm them with Sharps and Spencer rifles. The Secretary agreed to investigate the "practicability" of furnishing 5,000 mules to Rousseau's division on 17 August.[68] This began another inquiry by BG Meigs as to where the horses and mules were that he had already sent to MG Rosecrans. Between 17 August and 4 September, 18 separate telegraph messages passed between Washington, Cincinnati, Louisville and Stevenson trying find out the numbers of animals already provided and what had become of them.[69]

BG Meigs, who no doubt already knew the answers, found that a total of 27,707 horses and 20,396 mules were transferred to, captured by, or purchased by the Department of the Cumberland between 1 December 1862 and 17 August 1863.[70] LTC Hodges also reported that the depot at Nashville housed 5,409 mules that were not assigned to units. BG Meigs asked LTC Hodges to explain why they could not be used for MG Rousseau.[71] LTC Hodges' response was that these mules were used to exchange out broken down mules already with the army and they could not be spared for MG Rousseau.[72] Secretary Stanton had by then ordered BG Meigs to purchase the mules and BG Meigs informed MG Rosecrans on 28 August that funds would be provided to purchasing officers to procure the animals.[73] Yet again, BG Meigs was forced to become personally involved in forcing the commander and the Chief Quartermaster of the Army of the Cumberland to account for the resources they had been provided and explain in detail how those resources were being used and why they needed more. In the end, the authorization for the purchase of 5,000 mules at $125 a piece for a total of $625,000 was approved, but at a cost to MG Rosecrans in respect and a waste of his and his staff's time in an endeavor that would not assist him in the present campaign and in the end never came to fruition.[74]

As the Army of the Cumberland moved forward and the numbered corps and most of the cavalry left middle Tennessee, MG Rosecrans assigned MG Gordon Granger's three-division, 18,747-man Reserve Corps responsibility for garrisoning and securing the depots and lines of communication in the army's rear.[75] MG Granger telegraphed BG Garfield on 23 August that, "My command is terribly scattered," which it certainly was.[76] He was covering north of Nashville at Clarksville and Gallatin, to Nashville, then south to Murfreesboro and Tullahoma west to Columbia and down to Decatur, Alabama. He put BG Robert S. Granger in command of Nashville proper, where he stayed throughout the Chickamauga Campaign. BG James D. Morgan was in the west sector down to Decatur and BG James B. Steedman's division was garrisoning along the N&C from Murfreesboro to Cowan. [77] He had minimal cavalry support so he requested on 24 August to be allowed to immediately outfit several new Tennessee cavalry regiments under the command of BG Alvan C. Gillem that were in Nashville. He then learned that these units might also be pulled from him and protested that, "it will be impossible to guarantee the supplying of your army unless you send me two or three good regiments of cavalry to protect the lines of communication."[78] MG Granger telegraphed on 3 September that if the 5th Iowa Cavalry was pulled from him, no mounted troops would patrol the railroad from Murfreesboro to the Tennessee River and that, "Guerrilla bands and bands of thieves were organizing in all quarters."[79] MG Rosecrans' response was to tell him to organize patrols by infantryman garrisoning the rail line.[80]

On 4 September, BG Morgan was ordered to come east and garrison the Stevenson area and MG Granger was told to leave only minimal troops in his Middle Tennessee garrisons and bring himself and as many troops as possible to Bridgeport.[81] By 5 September he had 8,500 men in the area, leaving approximately 10,200 men to secure Middle Tennessee.[82] MG Granger also had the services of COL C.R. Thompson's Colored Volunteer Regiment in his sector. This unit was based at the Elk River Bridge but was broken into battalions, apparently to serve mostly as laborers, which MG Rosecrans had a critical need for along the railroad and at the depots.[83] On 9 September, MG Granger was put in command of everything north of the river.[84] The almost impossible mission assigned to MG Granger brought this plea from him on 10 September, "Have you any pity for the rear?"[85]

The order putting all the areas north of the Cumberland Plateau, and then of the river, under MG Granger's control did not define his authority and responsibilities. MG Granger and his subordinate commanders began making changes contrary to the plans and procedures of the logistical officers operating out of Nashville, probably due to orders coming to them but not to the logistical officers. The conflict had become so great that on 1 September, General Order 215 was issued spelling out the duties of each quartermaster officer in Nashville. It was followed on 2 September with an order directing district and post commanders to supervise logistical operations in the rear but through, "the regularly appointed officers of the depot and railroad for the purpose of insuring promptness and dispatch."[86]

The haphazard manner that MG Granger was assigned his tasks, the lack of guidance and support, and the vulnerability of the lines of communication is surprising. The fact that a plan for the security of the lines of communication was not available from the army commander before the move across the Cumberland Plateau took place is inexcusable. MG Granger had too few troops and too large an area to secure even before he was ordered to strip Middle Tennessee of troops. MG Rosecrans also had to take time during the movement on Chattanooga to write instructions to his officers securing the lines of communications, spelling out how to conduct their patrolling, defenses to be built and reports to be forwarded.[87] This should have been disseminated a month prior. The weeks spent around Tullahoma and Stevenson were not spent anticipating the new problems that would arise in the army's rear as it moved farther from its base of supply. It was a planning deficiency by MG Rosecrans and his staff that forced MG Rosecrans to divert his attention from the active campaign and become involved in petty matters far in the rear.

In his 15 August order to the corps laying out the move across the Plateau, MG Rosecrans ordered each division commander to divide his trains into three sections. The idea was to have them on a continuous cycle of one section issuing supplies to the troops, one enroute to or from the troops, and one getting its supplies replenished at the closest depot. The idea was to keep the huge trains from clogging the roads behind the divisions and also keep a constant resupply operation going, though this became more difficult as the units got farther from the rail heads and had numerous natural obstacles between them and the troops. He also ordered the divisions to "see that plenty of horseshoes, nails, ropes, and paulins are taken along to replace breakages, and furnish means to improvise boats for crossing streams and even rivers."[88]

BG Wood informed the XXI Corps headquarters on 15 August how he set up his transportation assets, certainly a concern of MG Crittenden after his corps performance in Tullahoma. He wrote that he had allotted one wagon per 75 officers and men, one wagon for field and staff requirements, one wagon for the medical department, and one for the quartermaster per regiment. This allowed him 49 wagons for his division supply, or quartermaster, train. He did not say the number of wagons in his ordnance train.[89]

MG McCook, in an attempt to stop the problems he faced during Tullahoma from happening again, issued specific directions to his units regarding wagons. He ordered:

> The number of wagons for the transportation of camp equipage, baggage, etc., in this corps will be reduced to the following allowance: for a regiment of infantry, three wagons; for a battery of artillery, three wagons; for a headquarters of brigade, three wagons; for a headquarters of division, ten wagons.

He was very specific about what could and could not be carried at each level, to include only two extra tent flies for a regimental headquarters, one wagon filled with blacksmith tools and supplies at each brigade, and four of the wagons at division filled with at least 800 pairs of shoes for the men. MG McCook also wanted all ammunition currently carried in company wagons to be sent to the division ammunition train for transport, which was to carry enough for 110 rounds per man and 250 per gun. He concluded with a telling paragraph:

> All means of transportation in excess of the above allowances will be organized under the direction of the corps and division quartermaster into division supply trains, and each division supply train will be subdivided into sections, with a sufficient number of wagons in each section to carry six days substantial rations for the division. Each section will be placed in charge of a quartermaster or other commissioned officer detailed from the division.

MG McCook forwarded a copy of his order to MG Rosecrans and stated that:

> By the system herein adopted I will be able to carry twenty-four days' full rations and three days' forage in my wagons, besides the rations carried in the men's haversacks. If it is necessary to carry a full supply of forage in the wagons, I can move my corps with fifteen days' full rations and forage. It is not designed as a general rule to move the entire supply train with the troops, but to have it brought up by sections, as the supplies are needed.[90]

His order called for three sections with six days of rations in each which totals 18 (additionally, the men could be carrying up to three days in their packs), how he came up with 24 days is not explained; no other wagons were authorized to carry commissary stores. This did not mean that a division had 18 days rations with them; it only meant they had the transportation available to bring them 18 days worth. The staggered sections still had to make their way in slow moving trains to the fast marching and riding troops.

Just as in the Tullahoma Campaign, the "excess" wagons never actually left the corps; they were taken from the regiments and brigades and ended up in the division trains. The size of the logistical "tail" of the army never was reduced, only shifted. The new rule of using the trains in sections was meant to keep fewer wagons with the divisions at any one time, but was impractical in the bottle necks, rough roads, mountains and distances that were encountered in the Chickamauga Campaign. The ordnance train was kept with the divisions; since the ammunition was not used on a daily basis, no rotation of wagons was needed. No accurate numbers of wagons in the supply or ordnance trains is found in the monthly inspection reports or the Official Records for the Chickamauga Campaign, but it must have numbered several hundred for each of the corps. The Army of the Cumberland's reserve ammunition train, which did not arrive in Stevenson until 10 September, by itself numbered 800 wagons.[91] The army had an enormous, slow-moving logistical "tail" trailing it as it moved across the mountains south of Chattanooga; it had the potential to be helpful or a hindrance to an army deep in enemy territory.

Reports had come into the army from spies about the crops that would be available in east Tennessee and north Georgia. (Allowing time for the corn to ripen was one reason MG Rosecrans gave in his post-battle reports for not advancing earlier.)[92] A report by an "R. Henderson" in the 8 August Operational Journal of the XIV Corps stated;

> The wheat and oat crops are unusually good, but are being fast consumed by the army (Confederates). The corn crop is good, but will be short, from the fact that a less quantity has been planted than usual, and not well tilled. The hay crop was only moderate, and for miles around Chattanooga has been consumed, or nearly so.[93]

The procurement of supplies in the local area, or foraging, was discussed in General Order 200 issued on 15 August by MG Rosecrans. In it, he stated;

> Where it is possible, commanders of troops will send in advance notice to the inhabitants of the section from which they intend to draw supplies of the kind and quantity required and the points at which they will be received, informing them at the same time that, to avoid the evils consequent upon the customary mode of foraging, to insure to themselves prompt payment or proper vouchers, it will be necessary that the inhabitants themselves should provide and bring the supplies to the points indicated, or collect and give notice where they can be had and why they cannot be delivered at the specified place. . . . When encamped in an inhabited country commanders will establish, when practicable, markets, to be held at suitable times at designated points near the picket lines, to which the inhabitants of the country will be invited to bring, for sale or barter, vegetables, fruits, forage, and all supplies required for the use of the army.[94]

The forage available locally varied greatly as the army moved east. On top of the mountains, it was limited due to the poor soil and small farms. In the valleys, it was often plentiful. BG Van Cleve, of the XXI Corps, reported in the Sequatchie Valley on 26 August, "an abundance of wheat being reported in the valley,"[95] and on 1 September that, "corn and potatoes are abundant."[96] MG Negley, of the XIV Corps, reported on 2 September from Moore's Spring, Alabama that, "river bottoms abounding with nearly ripened corn. . . . Hogs are plenty, but will require lard to fry the meat. The farms are well stocked with cows, calves, and a few sheep."[97] The amounts of forage varied from valley to valley, often due to previous foraging by Confederate forces. MG McCook reported on 4 September from Valley Head, Alabama in Lookout Valley that, "I have but little forage in this valley."[98] Yet MG Negley would report on 6 September in the same valley, only farther north near Stevens Gap, that there was, "plenty of forage in the vicinity."[99] On 15

September, MG McCook reported about BG George Crook's cavalry division near Dougherty's Gap on Lookout Mountain, "Unless he can go into the valley (McLemore's Cove) I do not see how he is going to subsist his animals, for there is not a particle of forage on the mountains."[100] On 3 September, MG Rosecrans, finding animals available in the region, asked permission from MG George Stoneman, the Chief of the new Cavalry Bureau in Washington which was responsible for purchasing and inspecting horses and mules for the armies, if LTC Hodges could be authorized to buy animals "in this country." MG Stoneman was still inquiring as to numbers of horses needed when the battle was fought.[101]

With vegetables, fruits and animals available on the march routes, hungry soldiers were going to desire to make use of them to supplement their bland issued rations. It may have been possible to enforce MG Rosecrans' order on organized "markets" to protect local citizens in an area long occupied and patrolled, but in areas where the corps were passing through or encamped just a short time, it would be impossible and many complaints of unauthorized foraging were reported.

On 27 August MG Palmer, of the XXI Corps, issued a circular to his division about the straggling, foraging and pillaging of the soldiers. To stop it, no one could leave the camp without a pass issued by the provost marshal and any party leaving camp had to be led by a commissioned officer who would be held accountable for its actions.[102] BG Baird of the XIV Corps issued an order on 8 September condemning the unauthorized foraging by his men of, "hogs, cattle, potatoes, and other property of citizens along our line of march." He wanted officers and non-commissioned officers to investigate incidents when they arose. If the individuals could be ascertained, they should be punished; if only the company could be found, the company would have its pay withheld; if only the regiment; then the regiment's pay would be withheld. A new problem arose for BG Baird to complicate the situation. He was ordered to subsist the animals in his command from the countryside due to the problem of getting the supply wagons to the units (to be discussed later in this chapter). "We are directed to forage our animals upon the country through which we pass." BG Baird then spelled out the process to obtain forage: first a supply must be located; then the regimental and battery quartermasters had to request from the brigade quartermaster permission to collect the forage; memoranda had to be prepared as to where and what was gathered and receipts for payments or vouchers provided to the farmer were to be retained by the brigade.[103] The unauthorized foraging was still a problem in the XIV Corps on 15 September when MG Thomas issued an order to his division commanders to see that:

> A more strict enforcement of orders is maintained in your command in regard to foraging, directing quartermasters to see personally that a supply of forage is procured daily with their teams, on proper vouchers given therefore. Individual foraging must be discontinued, as it gives the widest latitude for depredations, demoralizing the troops, and keeps a crowd of citizens at headquarters complaining and seeking renumeration, consuming valuable time which should be devoted to other purposes.[104]

The issue probably was not settled by the time the Battle of Chickamauga was fought on 19 and 20 September. The widely dispersed columns, ample forage in the region, and approval of junior officers and noncommissioned officers made foraging a common and uncontrollable aspect of the campaign. It also was necessary because of the issues with resupply from Stevenson. Foraging helped keep the army fed during the invasion of north Georgia, something MG Rosecrans could not do with his normal supply system.

The Army of the Cumberland began its move to cross the Tennessee River on 28 August. That evening, COL Hans Heg's XX Corps brigade moved to Caperton's Ferry, four miles east of Stevenson and 10 miles south of Bridgeport. On the morning of 29 August, COL Heg crossed soldiers in 50 pontoon boats to secure the far side, then assisted the men of the Pioneer Brigade in laying a 1,254 foot pontoon bridge in just 4 ½ hours. Two division's of MG McCook's XX Corps and one from MG Thomas' XIV Corps crossed here.[105]

On 1 September, MG Sheridan had the 1st Michigan Engineers and Mechanics build the "A" frame trestle bridge at Bridgeport, using the materials they had previously gathered. The bridge was ready to cross troops by the morning of 2 September. MG Sheridan followed one division of MG Thomas' corps across this bridge.[106]

Two additional crossing sites were used upstream from MG Sheridan's bridge. Five river miles north of Bridgeport, BG John Brannan's XIV Corps division crossed the river at the mouth of Battle Creek using poplar log dugouts and rafts. Six river miles north of Battle Creek, BG J. J. Reynolds' division of the XIV Corps and most of MG Crittenden's XXI Corps crossed their troops using captured boats and flatboats at Shellmound, Tennessee on 30 August. They were able to cross 400 infantrymen an hour or seven or eight wagons, with teams, in a trip. By 4 September, virtually all of MG Rosecrans' troops, minus the Reserve Corps and part of MG Crittenden's forces still threatening Chattanooga from the north side, were across the river.[107]

The next obstacle the Army faced was Sand Mountain, less than two miles from the river and which rose 2,200 feet from the river valley. There were three unimproved roads that passed over the mountain. To alleviate congestion on the roads and speed up the progress across the mountains so as to get south of Chattanooga (thereby threatening GEN Bragg's lines of communications with Atlanta), each corps took a different route over the mountain ranges. MG Crittenden's XXI Corps took the northern route of the railroad that passed down the valley created by Running Water Creek between Sand and Raccoon Mountains, then on to Whiteside, Tennessee. MG Thomas' XIV Corps took the middle route five miles south of MG Crittenden. He went up Sand Mountain at Moore's Gap, passed by Lively's Mill, and descended the mountain at White Oak Gap and entered Lookout Valley at Trenton, Georgia. Ten miles south of MG Thomas, MG McCook's XX Corps ascended the mountain up Caperton's Ferry Road, crossed over the broad, flat top of the mountain and descended into Lookout Valley and moved to the village of Valley Head; these movements were completed by 6 September. They encountered only Confederate skirmishers and deserters along the way.[108]

MG Rosecrans had received numerous reports from deserters and locals that the Confederates were evacuating stores and equipment from Chattanooga and he became convinced that GEN Bragg was abandoning the city and fleeing south toward Atlanta.[109] To cut off the retreating Confederates and force a decisive battle, MG Rosecrans ordered MG Stanley on 3 September to move from the Valley Head area across Lookout Mountain, via Winston's and Henderson's Gaps, to Alpine and then drive east with his Cavalry Corps to try and cut the railroad near Rome, Georgia. He ordered MG Crittenden to push forward through Wauhatchie, Tennessee, around the northern lip of Lookout Mountain and enter and occupy Chattanooga. MG Thomas was to move south of Trenton and then east across Lookout Mountain and descend at Steven's Gap into McLemores Cove, a "V" shaped valley formed by Lookout Mountain and Pigeon Mountain to the east. MG McCook was to move across Lookout Mountain using the same route MG Stanley had taken and go to Alpine to support the cavalry. When these moves occurred, the corps were no longer in supporting distance of each other with MG Thomas's position being 20 miles south of MG Crittenden and MG McCook 20 miles south of MG Thomas.[110]

As the corps moved across the river and mountain ranges, the division wagon trains were trying to do the same. The corps commanders were making the unrealistic claim to headquarters that they were carrying 25 days' rations with them in their trains as they crossed.[111] As previously discussed, this was disingenuous at best. With the supply trains being broken down into three sections, each carrying 6 days rations, 25 days of rations could not be with the corps at any one time. BG A. Baird, of the XIV Corps, advised his brigade commanders that they would have to cram an additional 10 days of supply in the regimental wagons to try and meet the order for 25 days of rations on hand.[112] At least one division, MG Sheridan's, crossed the river with no supplies issued to the troops and, with their trains on the far side of the river drawing supplies and waiting to cross, MG Negley had to temporarily provision them.[113] Believing the corps had 25 days supply was an unrealistic expectation that would become an issue within a few days of crossing.

The pontoon bridge at Caperton's Ferry held up well during the crossing but the bridge at Bridgeport had problems. The "A" frame supports sitting on the riverbed had the dirt at the bottom of the posts washed away. This caused 700 feet of the bridge to collapse on 2 September with one mule drowned and the contents of several wagons damaged. It was repaired and troops and trains were again moving across by 3

September; other less serious damage was done in the following days and quickly repaired.[114] MG Rosecrans sent a dispatch to MG Granger on 9 September which contained in it instructions concerning the bridges. MG Rosecrans told him to, "put the two bridges in order at Bridgeport" and later, "take care of Caperton's Ferry pontoon-bridge."[115] CPT Patrick O'Connel, the new commander of the Pioneer Brigade with BG Morton's departure, stated in his report of the brigade's time at Bridgeport (31 August-14 September) that they helped construct MG Sheridan's bridge on the 1st and also built an additional trestle and pontoon bridge and another pontoon bridge (probably with LTC Hunton's newly constructed pontoons) along with fortifications.[116] By 13 September, MG Rosecrans' units had four bridges available at two sites to link them with their base of supply at Stevenson. (The Caperton's Ferry pontoon bridge was dismantled and paddled north to Battle Creek and reassembled on 17-18 September.)[117]

The trains of the divisions crossing at Caperton's Ferry and Bridgeport naturally followed their units across the same bridges. The divisions that crossed north of the bridges at Shellmound and Battle Creek would only bring a few of their wagons, probably just the regimental wagons, across on rafts or ferries. These units were ordered to send their trains south to Bridgeport to make the crossing, making that crossing point a busy bottleneck across the river.[118]

The roads the units encountered when they reached the mountains were unimproved and rutted dirt tracks, many nothing more than bridle paths. MG J. J. Reynolds reported to the XIV Corps headquarters on 4 September, "roads horrible."[119] MG Thomas wrote in a dispatch to headquarters, "I find the road up the mountain rough and quite difficult to get heavily loaded wagons and artillery up."[120] Huge rocks were imbedded in the road making it extremely rough. The road was just a narrow cut against the mountain in places and several wagons of MG Negley's division came too close to the edge and toppled over. CPT Alfred Hough, an aide to MG Negley, wrote:

> Our division was all of one day and night in ascending the mountain, not more than two miles certainly. . . . This ascent was finally made though we lost some wagons and several fine artillery horses, which dropped dead in the road.[121]

Some wagons had six men detailed to them; the men ran fence rails through the wheels and all but carried the wagons up while the horses pulled. [122] MG Thomas wrote to MG Rosecrans from Stevens Gap on 13 September describing the routes over the mountains:

> The roads to this point from Caperton's Ferry and Bridgeport are the most difficult ever passed over. The ascent and descent on both the Sand and Lookout Mountains average about 1 ½ miles in length, over each one of which is absolutely necessary to double teams in ascending, in order to get loaded wagons up; and by two of the passes it is an exceedingly difficult manner to ascend in double teams.[123]

MG Granger reported on 14 September as he was approaching Chattanooga, "We have been delayed in consequence of bad roads. Many of the wagons are smashed to pieces, and hundreds of shoes torn from the feet of our animals."[124] The army tried to improve the roads as best they could by prying out boulders and filling in holes, but this had minimal effect on the crude roadways they were traveling.[125]

The thousands of wagons and ambulances that trailed the army had a particularly difficult time in this region. The marching troops could still make decent time, but the transportation assets that carried the vital ammunition, food and forage of the army could not keep up. To complete MG Rosecrans' plan on severing the Confederate line of retreat and defeating GEN Bragg's army in battle, he had to move quickly over the mountains and drive east to the Western & Atlantic Railroad. The slow moving wagons had to be present for the army to fight that battle and survive so far from their base of supply in

Stevenson. Once the infantry and cavalry units reached Lookout Mountain they were forced to wait for their wagons to catch up before they could proceed, thereby delaying the offensive and throwing the entire plan into disarray.

By the evening of 3 September, MG Crittenden had a division at Whiteside, MG Thomas had one at Trenton and MG McCook and MG Stanley each had one at Valley Head.[126] The lead units, while having difficulty with the roads and, amazingly, a lack of any road maps of the area, still had uncongested bridges and roads to travel over.[127] The units following did not have this luxury. As the divisions crossed over, they crossed, or tried to cross, their trains right behind the troops. If a division commander saw an opening, he drove his unit over the bridge, sometimes separating a division from its trains and causing delay on the far side.[128] When the Bridgeport bridge collapsed, it delayed trains from three of the five corps from getting across for a day. The fact that the corps did not each cross at separate points but were intermixed led to divisions having to pass each other across the river on the road between Caperton's Ferry and Bridgeport. This, and the steep ascent up Sand Mountain, made the clearing of the roads on the east side a slow process that backed up the crossing of several divisions and trains.[129]

By 5 September all the divisions of the Cavalry, XIV, XX and XXI (minus several brigades still opposite Chattanooga) Corps were across the river and in Lookout Valley.[130] The trains were another matter. As they ascended Sand Mountain, then crossed its plateau and descended, the trains were bunched up and delayed. MG Sheridan crossed the river on 3 September but only progressed to the top of Sand Mountain in the next two days due to the trains blocking his way.[131] His train did not cross the river until the fourth, along with 130 wagons of the cavalry corps train.[132] It took him until 10

September to reach Winston's Gap.[133] MG Crittenden reported on 4 September that, "none of the transportation up, and General Wood will be out of supplies tomorrow."[134] Having to send the division trains to Bridgeport, and the traffic jam there, meant the three days rations in the soldiers' haversacks were all they had, because resupply was not yet possible.[135] MG Stanley reported on 3 September that his train was not expected at Valley Head until the fifth; even then it was only part of it.[136] BG Baird reported his XIV Corps division was not able to begin ascending Sand Mountain until 6 September, nine days after the first units began crossing the river.[137] BG Brannan of the XIV Corps reported that he was hoping to get his ammunition and supply trains up Sand Mountain by the evening of the sixth.[138]

MG Rosecrans recognized a problem with the trains early on. On 4 September he ordered that, "the trains of each division be placed under an energetic field officer, who shall be held responsible for their order and efficiency," in an attempt to speed up their progress and stop the army from bogging down in Lookout Valley.[139] BG Van Cleve, of the XXI Corps, appointed a LTC Vaughn as the field grade officer in charge of his division trains. LTC Vaughn was instructed to act in connection with the division quartermaster and commissary officers to push the trains forward. The trains were not allowed to follow behind their divisions because that would slow things up too much. One wagon per regiment and two per battery, along with the division ambulances, would travel directly with the division. The rest were behind all the marching units in what amounted to a massive corps train made of all the division trains.[140] The assigning of the field grade line officers did enable the trains to be led by an officer with greater rank to force things along, but in the end, the terrain and distances were the real problems. Whether the field grade officers made a difference is undetermined.

By 7 September, MG Rosecrans' army was sufficiently closed up that he began pushing his units across Lookout Mountain.[141] MG Crittenden was heading toward Chattanooga, MG Thomas through Stevens Gap to McLemore's Cove and MGs McCook and Stanley to Alpine, Georgia. The events that transpired with MGs McCook and Stanley were large factors in the eventual outcome of the campaign. Their distance from the rest of the army, the terrain, and their management of their trains kept the Army of the Cumberland in a precarious position while facing a reinforced and determined Army of Tennessee.

MG Stanley, who was quite ill and would turn over command of the corps to BG Robert Mitchell on 15 September, was ordered to take his cavalry toward Rome, Georgia and tear up the rail line to disrupt the Confederate retreat. MG Stanley realized he did not know if he had the proper equipment with his units to do this kind of work and began inquiring. On 5 September he sent a dispatch to COL E. M. McCook asking:

> The general commanding desires to know if you have any claw-hooks, crowbars, or any other means of tearing up a railroad track; also have you any torpedoes in your ordnance train for blowing up railroad bridges, culverts, &c? If you have not some of these instruments, and cannot make them here, they must be sent for to Stevenson immediately and hurried forward.[142]

COL McCook responded the same day that he had none of the equipment MG Stanley asked about nor anyone in his command that understood how to make a torpedo. The only explosives he had was the ordinary ammunition in his ordnance train, which, "has not yet come up."[143] This was certainly a major oversight with the commanders and logisticians in the Cavalry Corps but since they had never been used to tear up tracks, only protect them, it obviously was not equipment they normally had with their regiments. MG Rosecrans was also at fault for not ensuring they understood the missions they could be assigned in the coming campaign. The corps did not have the tools on hand, nor could they realistically return to Stevenson to obtain them, to effect the Confederate retreat as envisioned by MG Rosecrans.

MG Stanley was still near Valley Head and Winston's Gap (which was not a gap at all, only a point where a wagon road went up the mountain) on 7 September complaining that his force was too small to raid that far forward. He felt he could not hold the railroad long enough to destroy it since COL Minty's brigade was detached from him and he had to leave several battalions across the river to guard the Nashville & Huntsville Railroad.[144] MG Rosecrans wrote the same day that he thought an expedition could be mounted and directed him to push forward rapidly.[145] On 8 September, MG Rosecrans wrote him that since he could not manage to strike toward Rome he could have at least patrolled and picketed Lookout Mountain, which was not done. MG Rosecrans, who had done so much to build up this corps, wrote his corps commander that, "it is also a matter of regret to me that your command has done so little in this great movement."[146] MG Stanley finally pushed forward to Alpine on 8 September, saying he could not leave on the 7th due to a lack of horseshoes, with MG McCook's corps following behind him.[147]

Army headquarters had lost faith in MG Stanley's ability to control and lead his corps. BG Garfield wrote to MG McCook on 9 September, "in case General Stanley has left no arrangement for the movement and protection of his train, the general commanding desires you to attend to its safety and movement."[148] This is exactly what transpired. MG McCook reported that evening, "I am considerably trammeled by Stanley's train, but will order all the trains to follow after my troops, the supply trains preceding."[149] Immediately after sending this dispatch, MG McCook sent another, this one to COL Sidney Post, a brigade commander in BG Jefferson C. Davis' division. COL Post was being put in charge of moving and protecting all the division trains of the XX Corps and the Cavalry Corps. He was ordered:

> As soon as all the troops have passed up the mountain General McCook directs that you (with your brigade and the escorts left with the trains) perform the onerous and important duty of moving all the trains of the corps and the cavalry corps to the front, bringing up the rear. . . . Send all supply trains up first, in the same order as the divisions moved.[150]

COL Post diligently pushed the trains forward to the top of Lookout Mountain where he received orders in the evening of 11 September to only bring the supply wagons down the mountain to Alpine; the rest would stay in park on top of the mountain.[151] Before COL Post moved up Winston's Gap, he loaded 200 sick men into empty supply wagons and sent them back to Stevenson. The most telling aspect of this was that he described this train as "the only supply train [from the XX and Cavalry Corps] that returned to Stevenson."[152] The plan of having three sections of trains in constant rotation bringing supplies forward never happened, the sections bunched up and were pushed forward as best they could be.

On 13 September, MG McCook could finally report that his trains had ascended Lookout Mountain, though MG Sheridan arrived with no forage and with animals in a weakened condition. This was certainly a problem army-wide by this point and necessitated the order for the army to begin gathering forage locally. This same day the last of MG Stanley's trains arrived, though COL Post had to send a regiment back to

Sand Mountain to escort them, since no cavalry escorts were provided.[153] He had begun crossing the river on 29 August; 16 days later he was just beginning to close up his corps on the far side of Lookout Mountain ready to drive toward the railroad. MG Rosecrans' expectation of what his units could do over this terrain had been completely unrealistic.

MG Rosecrans' plan needed swift movements to drive into the retreating enemy before they could concentrate to meet him. At the same time, the Tennessee River and the Sand and Lookout Mountain ranges made any Union troops east of them isolated and vulnerable. They could not be resupplied in a timely fashion. It would appear that a minimum of four days would be needed to traverse the terrain from Alpine to Stevenson and another four to return. As the army moved farther east, this time would of course increase. MG Rosecrans' campaign plan, while admirable for its aggressive goals, was absolutely in conflict with the logistical realities on the ground. The army could not have fought more than one large battle with the supplies it left Stevenson with. By aiming for Rome as the point to cut the railroad, the army would have to cross another line of ridges and a major river. The distance from its railhead would be roughly 70 miles of extremely rough terrain. He would have become so isolated that any gains he made would have had to be relinquished as he would have to fall back closer to Chattanooga and get the steamers running to Bridgeport to bring his source of supply closer to the army. GEN Grant would later write in his memoirs, "I knew the peril the Army of the Cumberland was in, being depleted continually, not only by ordinary casualties, but also by having to detach troops to hold its constantly extending line over which to draw supplies, while the enemy in its front was constantly being strengthened."[154] Logistically, the campaign MG Rosecrans envisioned was bound to fail due to the transportation restraints during the

Civil War; he could not haul enough forage, food, and ammunition with him, or move it fast enough, to free himself from the need of a railhead or port long enough to do what he planned.

On 8 September MG Rosecrans learned that GEN Bragg had evacuated Chattanooga and ordered MG Crittenden to march into the city, leaving one brigade to garrison it while the rest of his corps headed south in pursuit of the Confederates. He had forces in Rossville, Georgia, approximately five miles south of the city, by 10 September.[155] The march to Rossville was not without logistical issues, yet again dealing with wagon trains. MG Palmer complained that his march was hindered by the trains of other divisions that, "moved at the will of the different quartermasters, and are intermixed very much. . . . I regret to say that it will be impossible to march with the rapidity desired by the general."[156] It would seem that even with the field grade officers assigned to the trains the problem of control and forward progress still was not worked out.

MG Crittenden assigned BG George D. Wagner's brigade to garrison the city and begin logistical improvements. Two things were pressing for him. First, since the railroad could not be opened for several months, was finding a steamer to haul supplies from Bridgeport to Chattanooga. COL Minty was sent north to the Hiawasee River to see if working steamboats were still intact there, but they had already been burned.[157] Back in August, COL Wilder had shelled the last two steamers docked in Chattanooga, sinking one and disabling the other.[158] The damaged steamboat was repaired by troops of the Pioneer Brigade (they also operated a sawmill to make lumber for construction projects). A steamboat engineer and river pilots were located in Chattanooga and the repaired boat made its trial trip on 18 September, too late to make an impact on the battle beginning to the south.[159]

BG Wagner's second mission was building a pontoon bridge across the Tennessee to open a secondary route back to Nashville. COL Wilder's shelling had also partially destroyed the Confederate pontoon bridge drawn up on the south side of the river.[160] On 12 September, MG Rosecrans ordered BG Wagner to build a bridge across the river. To do so, BG Wagner requested a company of engineering troops.[161] On 15 September, two companies of the 1st Michigan Engineers & Mechanics, under the command of CPT P.V. Fox, arrived with five wagons of tools to begin building.[162] By 17 September, the Michigan men, with assistance from the Pioneer Brigade, had half completed a trestle bridge like the one at Bridgeport, probably with salvaged Confederate pontoons in the center. A second bridge was constructed by months end.[163]

BG Wagner was also responsible for sending the empty wagons of the army that found themselves in Chattanooga back to Stevenson for supplies (most of these wagons were probably from the XXI and Reserve Corps.) He reported sending 400 back on 16 September and that he had on hand in Chattanooga a stockpile of 200,000 rations, with more wagons bringing in food and forage everyday.[164]

On 9 September, MG Rosecrans had accomplished his mission as assigned him by the War Department. Chattanooga and East Tennessee were free from Confederate occupation and the direct rail link to Virginia was severed. The campaign was called by BG Meigs, no big fan of MG Rosecrans, "not only the greatest operation in the war, but a great thing when compared to any war."[165] It was at this time that MG Rosecrans had to make a decision whether to pursue the Confederates or reconsolidate in Chattanooga and get the steamboats running to push forward his logistical base from Stevenson. MG Thomas is believed to have advised for reconsolidation in Chattanooga, but MG Rosecrans saw an opportunity to inflict heavy losses on a fleeing enemy and he ordered the pursuit continued.[166] It is easy to criticize in hindsight, but the simple fact is MG Rosecrans' army was very isolated and vulnerable and a pause to organize the supply line to Chattanooga would have been the most prudent thing to do. With this isolation and the knowledge that GEN Bragg was receiving reinforcements from Mississippi, east Tennessee, and Virginia, he must have understood that even if he won a battle in north Georgia he could never follow it up and would actually be in an even more vulnerable position since he could not easily replenish his supplies while the Confederates would grow stronger each day.[167] The bold action of crossing the mountains had won him Chattanooga, but the overwhelming logistical restraints he was experiencing should have made him realize that another operational pause, like the one at Stevenson, was absolutely necessary for long term success and should have been ordered.

GEN Bragg was not in hasty retreat back toward Atlanta. He was concentrating his army around Lafayette, Georgia. When MG Thomas ordered MG Negley to descend Lookout Mountain through Steven's Gap into McLemore's Cove with his division, GEN Bragg saw an opportunity to turn on his pursuer. On 11 September, the Confederates attacked MG Negley and BG Baird's divisions in a poorly coordinated effort. The Union divisions were pulled back to Stevens Gap and MG Rosecrans now understood that his isolated army corps were dangerously exposed to defeat in detail and he began issuing orders to concentrate the army. MG Granger was to bring what forces he could (three brigades) to Rossville, MG Crittenden was to come from Rossville and Ringgold to Lee

& Gordon's Mill, MG Thomas was to hold at Stevens Gap until MG McCook and MG Stanley/ BG Mitchell could move north from Alpine to Stevens Gap, then they would all join MG Crittenden at Lee & Gordon's. This movement was put in motion on 12 September.[168]

The units in the most difficult position were the XX and the Cavalry Corps. They had finally gotten most of their trains up Lookout Mountain and starting down to Alpine on 12 September, that same day the corps were ordered to move north to link up with MG Thomas.[169] This was difficult since they could not stay east of Lookout Mountain and head north because that would take them through Lafayette where the Confederates were concentrated. They would have to climb back up the mountain. MG McCook wanted to take the road on top of the mountain north to Dougherty's Gap which descended into the south end of McLemore's Cove, then go to MG Thomas.[170] With reports that Confederates were in the valley in force and since he had reports of bad roads on top of the mountain from Dougherty's to Stevens Gaps, he decided he had to continue west and descend the mountain at Winston's Gap then head north up Lookout Valley and approach MG Thomas from the rear.[171] It was a much longer route not just in miles but also because it called for ascending the mountain, descending, moving approximately 18 miles, then ascending the mountain and descending it again to exit at Stevens Gap into McLemore's Cove for the move to Lee and Gordon's Mill.

On the morning of 13 September the XX and Cavalry Corps began climbing the mountain, by 1130 hours most of the ammunition train was back up and the troops and regimental wagons were following close behind. With the crowded road, the movement to the top would not be completed until the evening of 14 September for the XX Corps trains, with the Cavalry Corps reaching the top on the 15th.[172] MG Thomas, who was given authority over MG McCook, ordered MG McCook to hurry two of his divisions to Stevens Gap with three days rations and 60 rounds of ammunition but with no, "camp equipage, baggage, ammunition, or supply wagons."[173] Each of the three divisions left one brigade back to assist guarding and moving their trains, BG William Lytle was temporarily in command until they reached Stevens Gap when COL Post took over again.[174]

There would be controversy between MGs McCook and Thomas' and MG Rosecrans' headquarters on the route MG McCook would take. MGs McCook and Thomas had both agreed that MG McCook should take the Lookout Valley route; headquarters felt he should have used the mountain road to cut down the travel time for his men and baggage. MG McCook's three divisions were all in Lookout Valley by the evening of 14 September with most of the baggage, supply, and part of the ammunition train still on top of Lookout Mountain. MG Rosecrans wanted him to climb back up the mountain and take the mountain road. MG McCook said that he cleared his route with MG Thomas and would not subject his troops to backtracking again. In the end, all but two brigades of MG Sheridan's division climbed back up the mountain and headed north; MG Sheridan moved north using Lookout Valley. The wagons moved north along the mountain top road toward Stevens Gap, though COL Post's orders were changed on 16 September to bring his wagons and any others he had collected near Winston's up Lookout Valley to cross over at Stevens Gap. The other trains would not have to move along the mountain road all the way to Stevens Gap. By 16 September the Union forces controlled McLemore's Cove and the trains descended to the valley at Dougherty's Gap and joined up with their units. The consolidation of most of the XX and Cavalry Corps with the XIV Corps was completed on 17 September, five days after MG Rosecrans realized the danger he was in. COL Post and a large portion of the XX and Cavalry Corps trains did not close with the army from the vicinity of Stevens Gap to Crawfish Springs until 20 September, the final day of the battle.[175]

The Battle of Chickamauga opened with skirmishing at Alexander's and Reed's Bridges on Chickamauga Creek, approximately five miles south of Rossville, Georgia. GEN Bragg's forces took the crossing points and MG Rosecrans was able to discern his next move quite clearly. GEN Bragg was attempting to get his forces across the roads connecting MG Rosecrans and his forces near Crawfish Springs and the Widow Glenn's home with Chattanooga to the north. If he cut the Lafayette and Dry Valley Roads, MG Rosecrans would have only a single road, which ran along the base of Lookout Mountain, to move four corps of men and materiel north to Chattanooga, a site he felt he had to hold. Because of this, on the evening of 18 September, MG Rosecrans ordered MG Thomas to pass behind MG Crittenden's corps and extend the Union flank to the north to counter GEN Bragg's expected attack in that area and protect the roads. This was accomplished during the night.[176]

The battle raged on 19 September starting at MG Thomas' northern flank, then to the center with MG Crittenden, and then the southern flank with MG McCook's forces. The army held against the Confederate attacks but sustained a large number of casualties. During the night the lines were contracted and MG Thomas was reinforced; he would eventually control all but 10 brigades of the army. With the shifting units during the morning, a confusing order was sent to BG Thomas Wood to pull his division out of line.

He complied and as his brigades were moving, LTG James Longstreet's Wing of the Confederate army attacked, driving right into the gap that BG Wood's division had just left in the southern end of the Union line. Two divisions on the Union right were crushed and the survivors, along with MGs Rosecrans and McCook, Crittenden, and their staffs fled north along the Dry Valley Road toward Rossville and Chattanooga. MG Thomas, with the support of MG Granger who marched to the sound of the battle late in the day, held the northern sector of the line in Kelly Field and on Snodgrass Hill until dark when he pulled out and headed back to Rossville.[177]

MG Rosecrans has been criticized for not retiring to Chattanooga during the night of 19 September. If his goal was to fight and preserve roads that were his lines of communication to Chattanooga, he had succeeded against a numerically superior enemy. Why not take advantage of the success and push on to Chattanooga to regroup, gather supplies and then regain the offensive? This was all but impossible since withdrawal in any semblance of order during the night in a heavy wooded area would be extremely difficult and dangerous. The wounded could not be gathered and evacuated; many would have to be abandoned. The thousands of wagons would clog the roads and keep the troops from being able to retire with the speed they would need to be successful. Lastly, they had held on the nineteenth, same as on the first day of Murfreesboro. They could win another victory like Murfreesboro the following day if GEN Bragg could be held back as he wasted all his offensive capability on bloody charges. Then the army and Chattanooga would be secure and breathing space and time could be gained for the Army of the Cumberland to refit and prepare for a new campaign. Such were the goals for fighting on the 20th. They obviously failed to be realized.[178]

Logistical support for the battle was mainly based around Crawfish Springs, a site four miles south of the Widow Glenn's cabin and south of the cross roads that led west to the Chattanooga Valley Road at the base of Lookout Mountain, north up Dry Valley Road, or east to Lafayette Road. Its main attraction to the army was the large spring pond located there across from a large brick plantation house. With the lack of creeks and

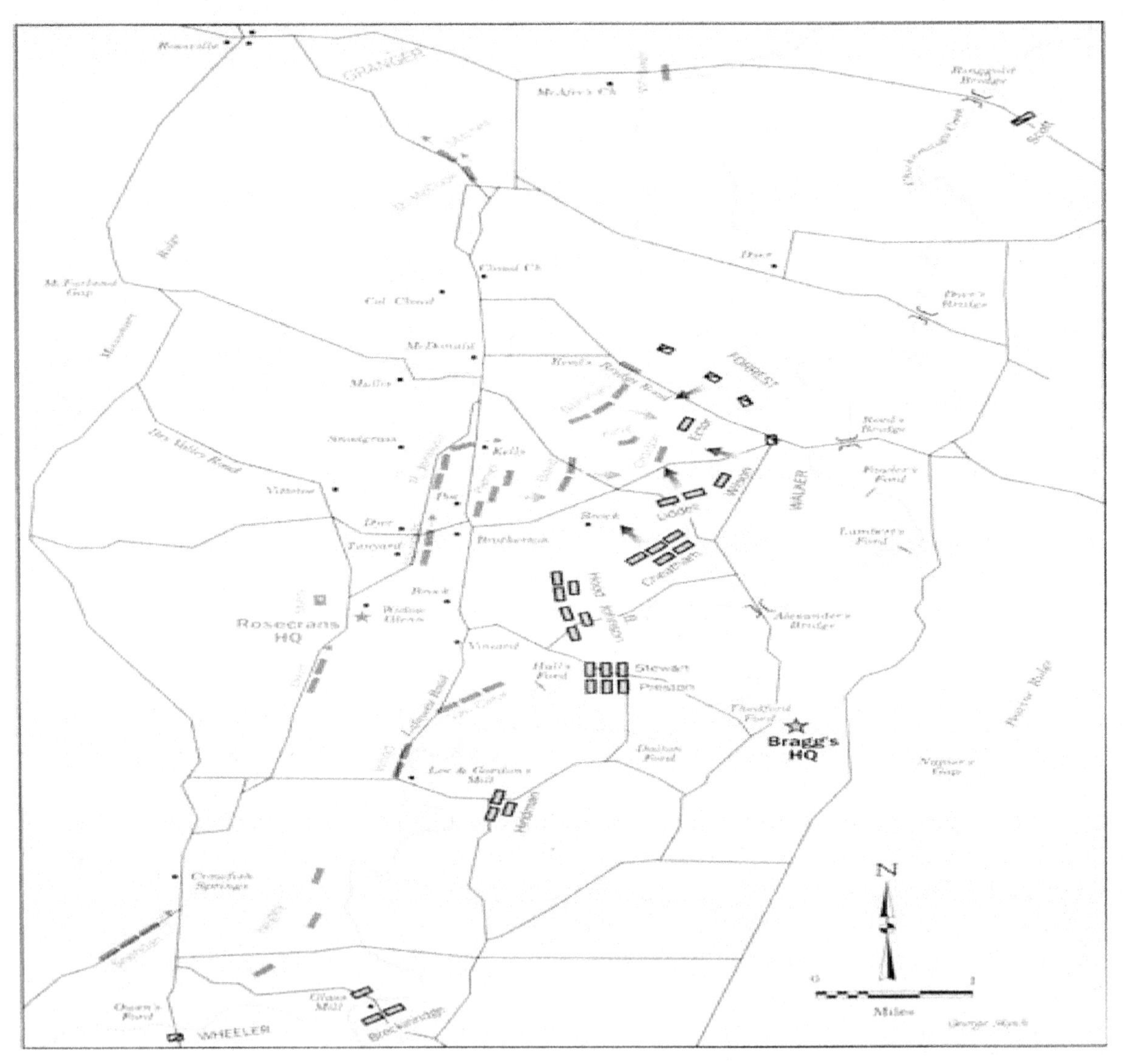

Figure 4. The Battle of Chickamauga: Midday on 20 September
Source: www.nps.gov

springs on the battlefield, this site would become important for the army, especially the wounded. For many men marching to the battlefield, this was the last site they filled their canteens until after the battle. [179]

Crawfish Springs was MG Rosecrans' headquarters on 17 and 18 September before he moved it up to the Widow Glenn's cabin.[180] MG Crittenden's trains were already located there and as the other corps passed, the medical wagons and the supply, baggage and many ammunition trains were left there. Dr. Perin, the army's Medical Director, selected Crawfish Springs as the main depot for the wounded. The division hospitals for the XX and XXI Corps were set up at or near there as well as two of the four division hospitals for the XIV Corps, an advantage because the medical staffs and supplies could be concentrated and shared instead of scattered over the battlefield.[181] The distance from the battlefield protected the site but also made the evacuation of the estimated 4,500 wounded on the first day a problem. All the local homes and outbuildings as well as the large hospital tents were soon filled with wounded. Those that could not be put under shelter were arranged in rows with camp fires built at their feet to warm them during the cold fall night and hot coffee and beef soup were also made available.[182] On 20 September, the distance from Crawfish Springs to MG Thomas' line was recognized as an issue and smaller hospital depots were established behind his lines.[183] The hospital of the 1st Division of the XIV Corps was placed near a spring at the Dyer house, behind the center of the Union line. The hospital of the 3d Division of the XIV Corps was set up at the spring near the Cloud house on the Lafayette road, one and a half miles north of MG Thomas' position.[184] Each of these sites used regimental and division medical stores, as well as the corps reserve stores, to supply and construct the field hospitals. The reserve supplies consisted of extra tents, blankets, sheets, pillows, shirts drawers, bandages, surgical instruments, mess-chests, concentrated milk and beef, liquor, and chloroform. In the XIV Corps these reserve supplies filled 15 wagons.[185]

The ambulance assigned to each regiment and battery, along with the ambulances maintained as a reserve in each brigade but often consolidated in the division trains, were responsible for evacuating the wounded from the collections points designated behind the units on the firing line by the regimental surgeons. The number of ambulances with the army is unclear. The monthly inspection report for July numbers do not match up with what the surgeons reported following the battle. The XIV Corps reported 132 ambulances, the XX 63 and the XXI 70. But the surgeons, apparently unaware of the issues the army commander was having with transportation, listed in their reports the following: Dr. Ferdinand Gross, the XIV Corps Medical Director reported 30 ambulances in each division train as well as one with each regiment and battery for a total of 180 ambulances; Dr. Jabez Perkins, the Medical Director of the XX Corps said he had a total of 105 available on 2 September; Dr. Alonzo Phelps, the XXI Corps Medical Director, reported 30 with each division train as well as one with each regiment and battery for a total of 136.[186] The grand total for just these three corps of the army was 421, not the 265 reported to MG Rosecrans. This certainly worked out well for the wounded on the battlefield, but made MG Rosecrans' job of managing his resources even more difficult since his units were purposely underreporting ambulances, and wagons, to keep him from forcing them to turn them in as excess.

On the morning of 20 September, the hospital at Dyer Field was being shifted to a more secure position farther to the rear. When the Union lines were broken, only one tent was left on the site to fall into the hands of the Confederates. Later in the evening the hospital at the Cloud house would also be captured along with 60 non-transportable wounded and three physicians.[187] Crawfish Springs was cut off from the army when the Union right flank was penetrated. The hospitals were being protected by BG Mitchell's cavalry and had time to pack up equipment and supplies and wounded to move them west to the Chattanooga Valley Road for transport north to Chattanooga. LTC Boyd, Chief Quartermaster of the XX Corps, and CPT Leech, Chief Commissary of Subsistence for the XX Corps, assisted the evacuation by providing empty wagons filled with straw to haul wounded.[188]

With the retreat of the army to Chattanooga, many of the more gravely wounded men had to be abandoned on the field. Dr. Perin states 1,500 were left in Crawfish Springs and a total of 2,500 were left on the battlefield as a whole. Medical officers were detailed to stay behind to continue treating the wounded. The XIV Corps detailed 19 officers, the XX had 11 and the XXI had 14 that stayed behind. The wounded were first taken to Chattanooga, then to a 1,500 bed General Hospital that was set up at Stringer's Spring north of the Tennessee River on 21 September. After the retreat to Chattanooga, a flag of truce was sent out which resulted in the return of 1,740 wounded men to Union lines. The total casualties reported by MG Rosecrans was 1,644 killed, 9,262 wounded, and 4,945 missing, and an additional 500 casualties predicted in the Cavalry Corps for a grand total of 16,351. This number of wounded would overwhelm any medical system that could be developed; the resources could not possibly be dedicated to properly care for so many wounded in such a short amount of time. The care they did receive is a testament to the dedication of the Medical Department, and fellow logistical officers, in the Army of the Cumberland. Their actions undoubtedly saved thousands of lives.[189]

BG Mitchell had been ordered to close up on Crawfish Springs on 19 September. He covered the fords across Chickamauga Creek keeping the Confederates from gaining access to the depot at Crawfish Springs, along with detailing a regiment to carry water in buckets and barrels along the line (the barrels were possibly the ones BG Wagner was ordered to collect in Chattanooga two days earlier.) COL Post was ordered to come to MG McCook's position on the morning of 20 September after sending much of the corps trains north on the Chattanooga Valley Road to a safe position. When he arrived in Crawfish Springs at 1300 hours, BG Mitchell told him the right flank was broken and BG Mitchell took control of COL Post's brigade. The Cavalry Corps and COL Post's brigade then covered the logistical trains as they packed up and, around 1700 hours, moved west to Chattanooga Valley Road enroute to Chattanooga. BG Mitchell was able to keep the Confederates at bay until everything that could be moved was and he also picked up a regiment's worth of stragglers and two cannon from the XX Corps he found along the way.[190] BG Mitchell's calm and decisive actions saved the majority of the trains of the army, enabling it to fight another day.

CPT Porter, Chief of Ordnance for the army, filed a sparse report which only listed losses of equipment and rounds expended in the battle and not his department's actions on the field. By the afternoon of 20 September, there was a shortage of ammunition on the battlefield. BG Garfield wrote to MG Rosecrans on the evening of 20 September that "nearly every division in the field exhausted its ammunition, got supplies, and exhausted it again."[191] MG Thomas was running dangerously low of ammunition during his stand on the 20th after his ordnance trains parked on the Dry Valley Road were overrun or carried off in the retreat of the right flank units. MG Granger's ordnance wagon's fortuitous arrival on the field with nearly 95,000 cartridges staved off disaster. These were soon issued to the XIV Corps divisions, but it was only a temporary fix. Luckily darkness came before the units were completely out of ammunition.[192]

CPT Porter reported on 1 October the ordnance and ordnance stores expended, captured, and lost in the battle:

Pieces of artillery captured (by Confederates)..........................36 (of 256 assigned to army)
Artillery carriages captured 36
Caissons captured...22
Limbers captured..20
Rifled muskets lost and captured......................................8,008
Spencer rifles lost and captured..70
Carbines lost and captured...350
Colt's revolving rifles lost and captured..............................22
Colt's revolving pistols lost and captured............................410
Cavalry sabers lost and captured.......................................305
Sets of infantry accoutrements lost and captured......................5,834
Rounds of artillery ammunition expended in firing.....................7,325
Rounds of artillery ammunition lost and captured......................2,550
Rounds of infantry ammunition expended in firing......................2,529,952
Rounds of infantry ammunition lost and captured.......................150,280
Rounds of cavalry ammunition expended in firing.......................121,000[193]

MG Rosecrans wrote in his report that this battle had 12,675 fewer rounds of artillery and 650,000 more rounds of musketry fired that at Stone's River the previous winter. This matches up with the comments from the surgeons saying there were a greater percentage of gunshot wounds vice artillery wounds than they normally saw following a battle, certainly due to the wooded terrain on the battlefield making artillery less effective than usual.[194] This immense expenditure and loss of ammunition in the battle had to be made up from the 800 ordnance wagons Assistant Secretary Dana mentioned as seeing in

Stevenson on 10 September.[195] Whether these wagons made it to Chattanooga by the 20th is unknown. If they had not, it is doubtful the Army of the Cumberland could have fought another battle the size of Chickamauga if GEN Bragg had been willing to press his hard won advantage.

LTC Hodges and LTC Simmons, the Chief Quartermaster and Commissary of Subsistence for the army, respectively, did not file reports following the campaign so everything to be learned about the losses in their areas must be learned from the monthly inspection report filed at the end of September (discussed later in this chapter.)

MG Rosecrans fled the field with the shattered divisions of the right flank and headed north up the Dry Valley Road, through Mc Farland's Gap in Missionary Ridge to Rossville. At the crossroads with the Lafayette Road, he discussed with members of his staff what he should do next, turn right and try to join MG Thomas who was still fighting or turn left and go to Chattanooga. He decided to go to Chattanooga and his main reasons for doing so were logistical. He wrote in his report:

> On consultation and further reflection, however, I determined to send General Garfield there, while I went to Chattanooga, to give orders for the security of the pontoon bridges at Battle Creek and Bridgeport, and to make preliminary dispositions either to forward ammunition and supplies, should we hold our ground, or to withdraw the troops into good position.[196]

He would also write, "It was to provide for the security of these trains (at Crawfish Springs and Chattanooga Valley) . . . and that they should be moved into Chattanooga after our right was driven back . . . that I directed special attention."[197] For these reasons, and physical and mental exhaustion and the shock of witnessing the crumbling of the right flank, MG Rosecrans left two-thirds of his army as they fought on the field with MG Thomas. MG Thomas withdrew to Rossville in the dark where rations and ammunition were forwarded to him and continued to Chattanooga on 21 September. Gen Bragg could have followed but his own army was in shambles and needed to reorganize and gather up the spoils left on the field by the defeated Union army. No immediate shortages existed in Chattanooga, besides forage, but the army had lost its offensive capability and was now outnumbered and isolated deep in the enemy's territory.[198]

This ended the Chickamauga Campaign. The following is the corps', minus the Cavalry Corps whose report is unavailable, and attached and detached units' monthly inspection reports for the month of September (see table 6.)

Table 6. September Inspection Report

30 SEP '63	XIV Corps	XX Corps	XXI Corps	Res. Corps	Detached Cmds	1st Mich. Eng. & Mechs.	Pioneer Bde (17 Sep)*	Total**
Men (Officers + Enlisted)-	*16,071* present + 12,271 absent 28,342 total	*9,597* present + 8,132 absent 17,729 total	*10,741* present + 8,055 absent 18,796 total	*11,484* present + 5,355 absent 16,839 total	*1,145* present + 2,349 absent 3,494 total	*721* present + 188 absent 909 total	885 total	*49,759* +36,350 86,994
Wagons-	525	210	367	138	63	32	NA	1,335
Ambulances-	136	54	63	12	6	2	NA	273***
Horses-	471	225	292	41	92	92	112	1,325
Mules-	2,227	1,225	2,178	818	354	82	NA	6,884
Tents-								
Hospital-	18	2	16	5	6	2	NA	49
Sibley-	25	0	0	0	0	0	NA	25
Wall-	434	38	231	128	61	32	NA	924
Bell-	16	1	19	18	1	68	NA	123
Common-	10	5	0	0	3	18	NA	36
Shelter-	6,417	2,135 1/2	4,676 1/2	2,029	1,414	20	NA	16,692

*Monthly report unavailable, partial report done on 17 September from *OR*, vol. I, part III, 716 used.
**With Cavalry Corps not listed, a complete listing of army personnel, animal and equipment losses cannot be determined.
***Reminder, corps surgeons reported higher numbers of ambulances than corps staff did in July- XIV had 180 ambulances, XX had 105, and XXI had 136 at start of battle.

Comparing this inspection report to the July report, the losses of equipment in the army can be seen. The Reserve Corps numbers do not match up to the level of combat they saw. Their losses in equipment are probably from converting over to Department of the Cumberland standards from Department of the Ohio standards during the summer. The best comparison can be done with the XIV, XX, and XXI Corps numbers from July and September (see table 7):

Table 7. July and September Inspection Reports Comparison
(July Returns – September Returns = Campaign Losses)

	XIV Corps	XX Corps	XXI Corps	Total Losses*
Men (Officers + Enlisted present)-	26,160-16,071= 10,089	13,894-9,597= 4,297	16,129-10,741= 5,388	19,774
Wagons-	725-525= 200	375-210= 165	470-367= 103	468
Ambulances- (Surgeon's numbers)	180-136= 44	105-51= 54	136-73= 63	161
Horses-	561-471= 90	799-225= 574	511-292= 219	883
Mules-	4,359-2,227= 2,132	2,186-1,225= 961	2,676-2,178= 498	3,591
Tents-				
Hospital-	52-18= 34	31-2= 29	42-16= 26	89
Sibley-	24-25= +1	19-0= 19	9-0= 9	27
Wall-	628-434= 194	224-38= 186	421-231= 190	570
Bell-	31-16= 15	2-1= 1	34-19= 15	31
Common-	5-10= +5	3-5= +2	2-0= 2	+5
Shelter-	13,294-6,417= 6,877	6,273-2,135.5= 4,137.5	8,204-4,676.5= 3,527.5	14,542

* The Cavalry and Reserve Corps, the Pioneer Brigade, Detached Commands and the 1st Michigan Engineers and Mechanics are not listed since the reports for the two months do not allow an accurate comparison; therefore, this is only a partial listing of the losses in the Army of the Cumberland. Personnel numbers include battle casualties and soldiers absent from disease. Items like wagons may not have all been captured by the Confederates but could have been destroyed on the roads during the march over the mountains and counted as a loss.

Outside of the appalling personnel losses, the losses of horses, mules, wagons and shelter tents are most significant. If, for example, each horse costs $125 and each mule costs $100, the Army of the Cumberland lost $110,375 and $359,100, respectively, for a total of $469,475 in just these three corps alone. Since the corps failed to list any ordnance or quartermaster wagons that directly supported them but were not in the authorizations allowed by the army commander, the actual number of horses and mules lost in these corps cannot be determined by the inspection reports. The 468 wagons lost had a total of 2,808 mules pulling them. How they lost 3,591 mules but only 468 wagons does not make sense. There should have been a loss of 598 wagons to account for the lost mules. The shelter half tents must have been rolled and placed on knapsacks or possibly set up behind the lines of battle. When the Confederates broke through, the soldiers must have lost these items as well as knapsacks and personal gear. The larger tents may have been set up for headquarters or still in wagons when captured.

The equipment, animals and men were not only expensive for the government to replace, but had to be replaced in a difficult geographic location in a city under a partial siege by GEN Bragg's army. It was also a windfall for the Army of Tennessee. Much of their old and worn out equipment could be replaced from the captured stores, a rare treat for Confederate armies in the Western Theater. It was a devastating defeat for the Union forces tactically, strategically and logistically and would sap the Army of the Cumberland's offensive strength until replacements and reinforcements began pouring in during October.

---

[1]Charles R. Schrader, *United States Army Logistics, 1775-1992: An Anthology,* vol. 1 (Honolulu, Hawaii: University Press of the Pacific, 2001), 23.

[2]James Lee McDonough, *Stones River: Bloody Winter in Tennessee* (Knoxville, Tennessee: The University of Tennessee Press, 1980), 28-29, 216-217.

[3]Larry J. Daniel, *Days of Glory: The Army of the Cumberland, 1861-1865* (Baton Rouge, Louisiana: Louisiana State University Press, 2004), 259-260.

[4]Ibid., 262-264; William M. Lamers, *The Edge of Glory: A Biography of General William S. Rosecrans, U.S.A.* (Baton Rouge, Louisiana: Louisiana State University Press, 1999), 275; and Micheal R. Bradley, *Tullahoma: The 1863 Campaign for the Control of Middle Tennessee* (Shippensburg, Pennsylvania: Burd Street Press, 2000), 44.

[5]Daniel, 259-260.

[6]Bradley, 45.

[7]Ibid., 53; Lamers, 277-278; *Campaign Atlas of the Civil War* (Department of History: United States Military Academy, 1980), map 39; and US War Department, *The War of the Rebellion: A Compilation of the Official Records of the Union and Confederate Armies*, Series I, vol. 23, part II (Washington, DC Government Printing Office, 1880-1901), 388 (hereafter cited as *OR,* Series I).

[8]Woodworth, 33-40; and Lamers, 279-287.

[9]*OR*, vol 23, part II, 446.

[10]Lamers, 279.

[11]Ibid., 281-282.

[12]*OR,* vol 23, part I, 523, 527, 528.

[13]Ibid., 528.

[14]Ibid., 530.

[15]Ibid., 442.

[16]Ibid., 483.

[17]Ibid., 514.

[18]Ibid., 467.

[19]Ibid., 581.

[20]*OR,* vol 23, part II, 478.

[21]*OR*, vol 23, part I, 474-475.

[22]*OR*, vol 23, part II, 549.

[23]*OR*, vol 23, part I, 418-424.

[24]Ibid., 580-582; *OR*, vol 30, part III, 701 and Lamers, 303.

[25]*OR*, vol 23, part I, 582-583; and George H. Turner, *Record of Service of the First Michigan Engineers and Mechanics in the Civil War, 1861-1865* (Kalamazoo, Michigan: Ihling Bros. & Everard: for Adjutant General's Office, 1903), vii.

[26]Daniel, 278 and *OR*, vol 30, part I, 50.

[27]Ibid.

[28]Lenette S. Taylor, *The Supply For Tomorrow Must Not Fail: Civil War of Captain Simon Perkins Jr., a Union Quartermaster* (Kent, Ohio: The Kent State University Press, 2004.), 121.

[29]Maury Klein, *History of the Louisville & Nashville Railroad.* (Lexington, Kentucky: University of Kentucky Press, 2003), 533.

[30]Lamers, 294.

[31]Taylor, 121.

[32]Taylor, 122; and Lamers, 300.

[33]Taylor, 124.

[34]Ibid., 123.

[35]Lamers, 301; and *OR*, vol 30, part III, 67.

[36]Map by COL William E. Merrill in 1865, Tullahoma, Chickamauga, and Chattanooga Campaigns Military Map, for Chickamauga and Chattanooga National Park Commission, printed 1896.

[37]George B. Davis, Leslie J. Perry, and Joseph W. Kirkley, *The Official Military Atlas of the Civil War* (Washington, DC: Government Printing Office, 1891), Plate CXII, number 3; Pamphlet, "Historic Fort Harker," produced by the Stevenson Depot Railroad Museum Board, Stevenson, Alabama, available from www.StevensonAlabama.com; and Eliza B. Woodhall, *The Stevenson Story* (Collegedale Tennessee: The College Press, Stevenson Depot Museum, 1982), 110-111.

[38]Woodhall, 105, 124; and Alabama Historical Commission Marker, *Union Army Headquarters ("The Little Brick"),* Stevenson, Alabama.

[39]*OR*, vol 30, part I, 222-223; and *OR*, vol 30, part III, 550.

[40]Flossie Carmicheal and Ronald Lee, *In and Around Bridgeport* (Collegedale, Tennessee: The College Press, 1967), 32-35, 37-39, 41-42.

[41]Richard E. Prince, *Nashville, Chattanooga & St. Louis Railway: History and Steam Locomotives* (Bloomington and Indianapolis: Indiana University Press, 2001), 6, 8.

[42]Lamers, 297.

[43]Carmicheal, 40.

[44]*OR*, vol 30, part I, 51.

[45]Ibid., 445-446, 51.

[46]*OR*, vol 30, part III, 87, 118.

[47]Ibid., 147, 153.

[48]Ibid., 11.

[49]Ibid., 56.

[50] Ibid., 68.

[51]Ibid., 85-86.

[52]Ibid., 507.

[53]Ibid., 173, 220, 235, 248, 255, 280; and Philip H. Sheridan, *The Personal Memoirs of P. H. Sheridan* (New York: DaLapo Press, 1992), 147-148.

[54]*OR*, vol 30, part III, 33

[55]Ibid., 84.

[56]Ibid., 171.

[57]Ibid., 297-298.

[58]Ibid., 407.

[59]Ibid., 480.

[60]Ibid., 499.

[61]Ibid., 530.

[62]Ibid., 33.

[63]Ibid., 279, 297.

[64]Ibid., 297.

[65]George B. Abdill, *Civil War Railroads: A Pictoral Story of the War Between the States, 1861-1865* (Bloomington and Indianapolis, Indiana: Indiana University Press, 1961), 151.

[66]*OR*, vol 30, part III, 111, 230, 342, 248; *OR*, vol 30, part I, 223; and Taylor, 122

[67]*OR*, vol 30, part III, 185, 280, 297; and Mark Zimmermann, *Guide to Civil War Nashville* (Nashville, Tennessee: Battle of Nashville Preservation Society, 2004), 11.

[68]*OR*, vol 30, part III, 62.

[69]Ibid., 62, 147.

[70]Ibid., 63.

[71]Ibid., 171.

[72]Ibid., 162.

[73]Ibid., 71, 199.

[74]Ibid., 71, 72, 199, 356, 357.

[75]Ibid., 37.

[76]Ibid., 140-141.

[77]Ibid., 192, 329, 330.

[78]Ibid., 155.

[79]Ibid., 238, 328.

[80]Ibid., 328, 329.

[81] Ibid., 351-352.

[82]Ibid., 373.

[83]Ibid., 81, 314, 353, 638.

[84]Ibid., 499.

[85]Ibid., 521.

[86]Ibid., 310-311.

[87]Ibid., 362.

[88]Ibid, 37.

[89]Ibid., 41.

[90] Ibid., 252, 253.

[91]*OR*, vol 30, part I, 184.

[92] Lamers, 294.

[93]*OR*, vol 30, part III, 48.

[94]Ibid., 34-35.

[95]Ibid., 177.

[96]Ibid., 289.

[97]Ibid., 299-300.

[98]Ibid., 345.

[99]Ibid., 384-385.

[100]Ibid., 652.

[101]Ibid., 322, 731.

[102]Ibid., 189.

[103]Ibid., 447-448.

[104]Ibid., 645.

[105]Lamers, 304.

[106]Sheridan, 147-148; and *OR*, vol 30, part I, 52.

[107]William G. Robertson, *The Battle of Chickamauga*, (Fort Washington, Pennsylvania; Eastern National, 1995), 14-15; and *OR*, vol 30, part III,132-133, 251, 233.

[108]Woodall, 133; Lamers, 306; and Merrill, Map, 1896.

[109]*OR*, vol 30, part III, 214, 322, 444, 469, 481.

[110]Ibid., 322-323; Lamers, 307; Robertson, 16; and Merrill, Map 1896.

[111]*OR*, vol 30, part III, 282, 305.

[112]Ibid., 283.

[113]Ibid., 300.

[114]Ibid., 296, 326, 333, 374.

[115]Ibid., 499.

[116]*OR*, vol 30, part I, 928-929.

[117]Lyman S. Widney, Diary, 17-18 September 1863, Sergeant Major, 34th Illinois Infantry, Unit Files, Kennesaw Mountain National Military Park.

[118]*OR*, vol 30, part III, 298, 347, 369.

[119] Ibid., 344.

[120]Ibid., 324.

[121]Daniel, 296.

[122]Ibid., 296; and Lamers, 305.

[123]*OR*, vol 30, part III. 600.

[124]Ibid., 636.

[125]Ibid., 449.

[126]Ibid., 321.

[127]Ibid., 326, 355, 409, 570.

[128]Ibid., 333.

[129]Ibid., 333, 374.

[130]Ibid., 361-362.

[131]Ibid., 368.

[132]Ibid., 346.

[133]Ibid., 490.

[134]Ibid., 348.

[135]Ibid., 369.

[136]Ibid., 331.

[137]Ibid., 383.

[138]Ibid., 385.

[139]Ibid., 340.

[140]Ibid., 372.

[141]Ibid., 412.

[142]Ibid., 375, 603, 653.

[143]Ibid., 375.

[144]Ibid., 344, 431-432.

[145]Ibid., 432.

[146]Ibid., 468.

[147]Ibid., 468.

[148]Ibid., 488.

[149]Ibid., 489.

[150]Ibid., 491.

[151]Ibid., 543.

[152]Ibid., 542; and *OR*, vol 30, part I, 506.

[153]*OR*, vol 30, part III, 572, 573, 603.

[154]Lamers, 315.

[155]*OR*, vol 30, part III, 451, 492, 493, 515.

[156]Ibid., 516.

[157]Ibid., 482, 553.

[158]Ibid., 113.

[159]Ibid., 531, 715; and *OR*, vol 30, part I, 929.

[160]Robertson, 14.

[161]*OR*, vol 30, part III, 582-583.

[162]Ibid., 651.

[163]Ibid., 715; and *OR*, vol 30, part I, 929.

[164]*OR*, vol 30, part III, 688, 715, 729.

[165]Lamers, 308-309.

[166]Robertson, 17; and Daniel, 299.

[167]*OR*, vol 30, part III, 381, 644, 691.

[168]Robertson, 18-19; *OR*, vol 30, part III, 535, 539, 541, 586, 598; and Glenn Tucker, *Chickamauga: Bloody Battle in the West* (Dayton, Ohio: Morningside Bookshop, 1984), 101, 105-106.

[169]*OR*, vol 30, part III, 572.

[170]Ibid., 598.

[171]Ibid., 599-600,

[172]Ibid., 603-604, 627-628, 637.

[173]Ibid., 604.

[174]Ibid., 605.

[175]Ibid., 629, 630, 677-678, 726; *OR*, vol 30, part I, 507; and Tucker, 105.

[176]Tucker, 110-113, 118-119, Merrill, Map 1896; and Lamers, 321-323.

[177]Robertson, 40-41, 45, 47-50; Lamers, 334-338; and Peter Cozzens, *This Terrible Sound: The Battle of Chickamauga* (Urbana and Chicago, Illinois: University of Illinois Press, 1996), 368-375.

[178]Tucker, 203-204.

[179]Merrill, Map 1896, Tucker, 118-119; and National Park Service Interpretive Marker, Crawfish Springs, Georgia, 2004.

[180]Robertson, 24.

[181]*OR*, vol 30, part I, 224.

[182]Ibid., 224, 495.

[183]Ibid., 225.

[184]Ibid., 260.

[185]Ibid., 259-261.

[186]Ibid., 494, 529, 619.

[187] Ibid., 261.

[188]Ibid., 225, 495.

[189]Ibid., 225, 262, 496, 620, 64.

[190]Ibid., 507, 893; and *OR*, vol 30, part III, 715, 744.

[191]*OR*, vol 30, part I, 145.

[192]Cozzens, 453.

[193]Ibid., 233.

[194]Ibid., 62, 227.

[195]Ibid., 184.

[196]Ibid., 60.

[197]Lamers, 354-355.

[198]Ibid., 360, 364-365.

CHAPTER 5

CONCLUSION AND RELEVANCE

> You will not find it difficult to prove that battles, campaigns and even wars have been won or lost primarily because of logistics.
>
> General Dwight D. Eisenhower, 1945

MG William S. Rosecrans, a man of intelligence and energy, was a poor logistician while most of the logistics officers who worked with and for him were more than competent at their jobs and did excellent service for the Department of the Cumberland and the nation. His interference and lack of advanced planning led to many logistical, and therefore strategic, operational and tactical, failures during the Tullahoma and Chickamauga Campaigns.

MG Rosecrans did find a great many logistical deficiencies when he took over the new Department of the Cumberland in 1862. He felt his personal intervention in many of the supply issues ensured they would be a priority to be filled by the War Department logisticians. This is certainly an excellent thing for a commander to do on an occasion, the power of his position can have a big impact, but turning to this technique frequently makes it just another request from one of many departments. He also failed to make a single long term goal for his army and set the logistical team on track to meet it. He asked the War Department for an item, horses for example, then when that request was processed and being delivered, often to the detriment of other armies, he came back with an additional request for the same item. This frequent changing of his forecasted needs, coupled with an inability to account for the materiel he'd already been given in his justifications for new items, made the War Department officials resentful and helped turn some from friends to enemies. The logisticians in the Department of the Cumberland made the Army of the Cumberland into a superbly equipped and supplied army in spite of the difficulties created by the interference of MG Rosecrans.

MG Rosecrans spent the six months following the Battle of Murfreesboro preparing for a fight he wanted to happen north of the Cumberland Plateau. When the Confederate army escaped over the Plateau and across the Tennessee River, he was not prepared to continue his invasion in a timely manner. The construction crews had the railroad open to the Tennessee River by 25 July, yet he was not able to move across the river until 29 August. The lack of foresight as to the number of railcars and locomotives that were needed to haul supplies to the forward logistics base at Stevenson was a massive failure on the part of MG Rosecrans and his Superintendent of Railroads, COL Anderson. The relationship of the Department of the Cumberland to the Louisville & Nashville Railroad Corporation also contributed to the problem. The L&N was allowed to disregard the needs of the army at Stevenson in order to make a profit. This is not entirely MG Rosecrans' fault, but he could have used his capital with the War Department on changing this situation instead of expending it on sporadic requests for mules and sabers. The railroad was his sole link with the power of the North, he had to use it to project that power on the South and he failed to do it properly.

The creation of a pontoon train under the new Pioneer Brigade prior to Tullahoma was a success story. The 700-foot bridge however was only meant to span the rivers of middle Tennessee, not to provide multiple crossing sites over the mighty Tennessee River. By not having the pontoons and bridging materiel already prepared and ready to be moved forward to the river in a timely manner, the eastern span of the railroad bridge at

Bridgeport was destroyed by the Confederates several weeks after the Union troops had arrived in Bridgeport. A rapid advance and crossing could have saved the bridge and put that part of the line back into use months before it actually was. Not having proper pontoon bridges for each of the corps meant that the two bridges that were built became choke points for thousands of wagons and began the delays that would become chronic in the days following the initial crossing.

MG Rosecrans recognized before and during the Tullahoma and Chickamauga Campaigns that the vast number of wagons with his army would slow its progress considerably while on the march. The orders he issued called for a reduction of wagons and for excess wagons to be turned into the quartermasters at Murfreesboro and later Stevenson. The lack of supervision by himself, his inspectors and the corps commanders enabled the divisions to keep the wagons they had culled from the regiments in their division trains and not count them in their inspection reports claiming they were owned and controlled by the quartermaster, ordnance and medical departments. This meant that no real reduction ever took place and that more than 5,000 wagons trailed after the army, making any marches turn into crawls. It was a terrible oversight by MG Rosecrans and a blatant disregard of orders by his subordinates that almost led to the destruction of his army.

The plan created by MG Rosecrans to invade northern Georgia was built on unrealistic expectations from the beginning. The geographical obstacles and large daily forage and sustenance needs called for a logistical base east of the mountains in order to continue an active campaign. He needed to occupy Chattanooga and open the river line with Bridgeport before he could expect success in fighting the Confederates but he failed to do this. By spreading his corps out over the rough Sand and Lookout Mountain ranges, he not only put them in positions where they could not support each other, but he made the distances traveled by the wagon trains too long to be done on a timely basis. The forces that descended the east side of Lookout Mountain in early September would not be capable of fighting a large scale battle for at least another week until their trains could close on their positions. In many ways, MG Rosecrans set his army up for failure at the start of the Chickamauga Campaign by issuing orders that were not based on the realities of the logistical situation.

The implications of the experiences of the Department of the Cumberland under MG Rosecrans for today's military lie in the areas of unit organization, staff coordination, and planning. The lack of any logistical units during the Civil War made the creation of a logistical system difficult to achieve. Manning the ever expanding logistical network was done by a few staff officers and noncommissioned officers, contract clerks and laborers, and detailed men from the ranks, a significant drain on combat power. The creation of logistical units in World War I to handle these duties made a dramatic improvement for the military and these units showed their full capability in their contributions in World War II. The creation of theater support commands and their subordinate logistical commands, each with commanders of commensurate rank with the combat arms forces, ensures that the units are utilized in the best way possible to support the maneuver units.

Today's logistical officers are represented on the staffs of division, corps, army and theater commanders, just like in the Civil War, but are seen in a multi-functional role. The senior logistician can be from any of the logistical specialties. This is done because logistics is not stove-piped where each specialty works within a narrow lane without coordination with other logisticians, but within a comprehensive view where each specialty enhances the others' abilities to provide materiel and services to the units they serve.

The logistical staffs are also able to create better support plans because they are integrated into the strategic, operational and tactical planning processes. Planning cannot be done in a vacuum but must have logistical planners involved from the beginning. Proper logistical support requires a great deal of lead time to put facilities, equipment and materiel in place before they are needed. This can only happen when the logisticians are an integral part of the planning process and able to present the logistical possibilities and restrictions inherent in a plan. If MG Rosecrans had had a logistical staff large enough to do planning and still carry out its day to day functions, and trained logistical units to support the maneuver units, the many logistical oversights of the Tullahoma and Chickamauga Campaigns probably would not have happened and the Battle of Chickamauga would never have taken place.

The military historian and theorist General Antoine Henri Jomini wrote about a conversation he had on whether new technology would affect the way wars were conducted:

> Happening to be in Paris near the end of 1851, a distinguished person did me the honor to ask my opinion as to whether recent improvements in firearms would cause any great modifications in the way of making war. I replied that they would probably have an influence upon the details of tactics, but that in great strategic operations and the grand combinations of battles, victory would, now as ever, result from the application of the principles which had led to the success of great generals in all ages; of Alexander and Caesar, as well as Frederick and Napoleon.[1]

While Jomini was writing specifically about tactics, his idea of certain aspects of warfare being timeless are certainly applicable to the area of military logistics. While technology has changed, making logistical support possible even in remote and isolated areas, this technology also brings with it additional burdens on the logistical system. For example, trucks and aircraft are excellent platforms for hauling supplies but the internal combustion and turbine engines found in trucks, aircraft, and armored vehicles also consume vast quantities of petroleum products and put additional strains on the logistical system (similar to the animal fodder in the Civil War.) Logisticians still analyze future areas of operation for the same natural and manmade geographic features that can assist in the delivery of supplies. Ocean ports, navigable rivers, improved road systems, and airports are all necessary for the transportation of the tonnage required for an army on campaign. Except for the airports, these requirements have not changed since the beginning of recorded time. The calculation of materiel requirements to delivery platforms available to distance to be traveled is done in the same way today as Alexander did it over a millennium ago and MG Rosecrans did it in 1863. The Iraq War is the most recent military operation to illustrate the timeless nature of strategic and operational logistics and the effect that logistics has at all levels of military planning.

The Iraq War of 2003 was fought against the regime of Saddam Hussein by coalition forces under the command of General Tommy Franks, the commander of Central Command or CENTCOM. His 3,000 person staff was split between MacDill Air Force Base in Tampa, Florida, and Doha, Qatar. On GEN Franks' staff the Joint 4 (J4), or senior logistician, was a major general which gave them sufficient authority and prestige to control the complex logistical system being set up to funnel troops, equipment and personnel to the Middle East.[2] This is in contrast to fragmented logistics organization and low ranking officers in MG Rosecrans' department.

The experience gained in the Gulf War in 1990 and 1991 and the constant rotation of battalions to Kuwait for exercises following that conflict right up to the Iraq War provided the logisticians of Central Command with an excellent template to follow in the build up to the Iraq War. Pre-positioned materiel and equipment was already in theater and in late 2002, large stockpiles of munitions, food, clothing, etc were being built up in warehouse complexes in Kuwait and Qatar in preparation for a possible invasion, a definite change in military policy from the Civil War when no preparation was done prior to the start of the conflict. The decision by the Kuwaiti Government to allow an invasion to begin from their country enabled this buildup to take place as well as upgrading and improving of airports, ports, and bases that would be needed during the upcoming troop deployment and sustainment operations. The ports around Kuwait City were the main delivery point for the supplies that entered the theater.[3]

The Army's 377th Theater Support Command (TSC) was the logistical command responsible for receiving the troops and equipment in theater, providing basic loads of ammunition, fuel and food, and resupplying the units as they rolled through Iraq. They not only supported the Army's V Corps, comprising the 3d Infantry Division (Mechanized) along with brigades from the 101st Airborne (Air Assault) and the 82d Airborne, the 173d Airborne Brigade and parts of the 4th Infantry Division (Mechanized), but also the 1st Marine Expeditionary Force, composed of the 1st Marine Division, a reinforced brigade called Task Force Tarawa, and the 3d Marine Aircraft Wing, and coalition forces, the largest being the British 1st (UK) Armored Division, composed of the 7th Armored Brigade, the 16th Air Assault Brigade, and the 3d Commando Brigade.[4] The 377th had 41,729 soldiers assigned to it in units with such varied specialties as medical, petroleum, personnel, movement control, trucking, maintenance, and supply.[5] The logistical system went from the theater support command units, to the Army corps support group and Marine forward service support group, to the Army division support commands, to the brigade forward support battalions, to the support platoons in each battalion down to the supply sergeants in each company.

Trucks were the main platforms for moving supplies in Iraq, but the 173d, which operated in the far north of the country, initially had to be resupplied by air, which is expensive and inefficient. The main routes of 450 mile invasion from Kuwait north to Baghdad were Highways 1 and 7, which follow the Euphrates and Tigres Rivers, respectively.[6] The combat units were free to maneuver off road as need be, but the supply convoys stuck mainly to the highways on their travels north and south for both speed and to reduce wear and tear on the wheeled vehicles.

The invasion began on 20 March 2003 and the coalition forces found that the troops of the Iraqi regular army units had no intention of being decimated like they had been in the Gulf War. Most of these troops deserted and returned to their homes. The main resistance the coalition forces faced was from Saddam's Ba'athist party members and Islamic fundamentalists, called Fedayeen, many of them foreigners who came to Iraq to fight Westerners. These troops were poorly organized, had no command structure or communications system, armed with only rocket propelled grenades (RPG's), Kalashnikov assault rifles and explosive charges, and recklessly exposed themselves to coalition gunfire on foot and in military and civilian vehicles and were killed by the hundreds by the armored columns as they raced north.[7]

The plan was for the British forces to take and hold Basra in the south (and open the port and rail line) and for the US armored columns to blast their way through the enemy divisions and towns north to Baghdad and surround it, then the light infantry forces would clear it block by block. Speed was essential to keep the enemy reacting to coalition moves.[8] With the lack of organized resistance, the progress north was much faster than expected. A sand storm kicked the fine silt found in the river valleys into the air on 23 March, cutting visibility and slowing the advance.[9] By 26 March, a more serious problem arose. The speed of the advancing columns outdistanced the supporting logistical trains which were needed to supply the fuel and ammunition that made the advance possible. The Marines were able to land a C-130 carrying a 5,000-gallon fuel bladder on the hard surface of Highway 1 to help refuel their vehicles. The 3d Infantry Division, which had a larger number of armored vehicles, was forced to wait for the tanker trucks before the advance could be continued. The halt to conduct the resupply operations lasted three days. A British observer wrote about the amazing capabilities of the U.S logistical support units at this time:

> The armor had halted with dozens of vehicles abreast in the first line and dozens more in the lines behind them. Suddenly out of the dust appeared every logistic vehicle you can imagine, tankers, water bowsers, ammunition trucks, mobile repair workshops, ration trucks. As they stopped, crews began connecting up hoses, hoisting pallets, throwing off crates. The contents were seized by the combat troops and disappeared inside the fighting vehicles as fast as they could be stowed. Sooner than you could imagine the combat echelon was re-supplied and ready to move forward again.[10]

As the armored units continued north, they did not clear the towns they passed through of enemy fighters. This meant that the unarmored and poorly armed supply and ammunition trucks, fuel tankers, ambulances had to drive up highways and pass through towns under a constant threat of attack by the enemy. The doctrine of the US forces was that the supply units would be operating in relatively safe rear areas during a conflict, this type of situation was not envisioned when the support units' equipment and armament were authorized during the Cold War. The town of Nasiriyah was an important crossing point on the Euphrates River for the Marines heading to the east side of the river and a site that the highway on the west side passed through before continuing on north. Since the town had not been cleared of the enemy, when the 507th Maintenance Company, which was attached to the 3d Infantry Division, took a wrong turn and ended up near the bridges in the city center, the enemy fighters were able to successfully attack it and destroy several vehicles and kill nine soldiers and capture six.[11] The vulnerability of the support units became a considerable problem during the war and, had the Iraqi forces been better organized and trained to take advantage of this weakness, would have caused the war to drag on much longer than it did.

When the 3d Infantry Division reached Baghdad, the 2d Brigade was ordered on 7 April to make a "Thunder Run" or armored raid into the heart of the city from the international airport (where the headquarters and support units were setting up) on the west side of the city. The brigade commander decided that when they reached the center of the city and occupied the grounds of the government buildings and Saddam's palaces, they would stay on site to signal to Iraqis and the world that Saddam's regime could not drive them out and was therefore defeated. The commanders understood that it would only be possible to stay in the city if they could get re-supplied once there. They planned to drive two tank battalions into the city and keep a mechanized infantry battalion at intersections along the line of communications to protect the supply vehicles. The support platoons, the units from the battalion headquarters companies that had the supply trucks and tankers, were particularly vulnerable in this urban fighting. While the armored units blasted through the enemy positions, the logisticians could do no such thing and became prime targets for the enemy small arms and RPG fire. The infantry battalion's 21 vehicle support platoon lost three ammunition trucks and two fuel trucks in devastating explosions when they went forward to resupply their battalion. Bradley fighting vehicles and armored HUMVEEs were assigned directly to the convoys for protection which enabled enough of the trucks and tankers to make it to the battalions for them to stay in Baghdad. Had the enemy understood the real weakness of the US units, they could have cut the logistical support (similar to the situation with BGs Forrest and Morgan in 1863) and compelled the battalions to retreat back to the airport and forced a long, drawn out clearing process to take place by the dismounted infantry units.[12]

The fighting during the war did not cause heavy US casualties, but there was an enormous expenditure of ordnance from 20 March to the pulling down of Saddam's statue at Firdos Square in Baghdad on 9 April. In the eight day battle to clear the town of Hillah, the 101st Airborne expended 1,000 Hellfire missiles from helicopters, 2,000 conventional artillery rounds, 114 rockets from multiple launch rocket systems (MLRS), and had 135 close air support missions flown to destroy 110 guns and rocket launchers, 287 armored vehicles, 800 other vehicles and numerous bunkers and firing positions.[13]

Throughout 2003, the 377th Theater Support Command created an amazing record of logistical accomplishment:

-Unloaded 165,000 pieces of equipment at the port

-Offloaded 47,000 containers and pallets of ammunition
-Processed 280,000 soldiers and marines and 90,000 tons of equipment in the theater
-Moved 20,000 convoys
-Handled 2,000 flights into theater
-Sorted and delivered an average of 244,444 lbs. of mail a day
-Transacted of $2.2 billion in cash purchases
-Level III medical care: 423 surgical procedures, 2,353 admissions, 8,470 outpatients
-Distributed 184 million gallons of fuel
-Fuel tankers traveled over 10 million miles
-Managed 2 trains per day on 500 miles of track to accomplish 15% of theater container moves[14]

As shown in the 377th statistics, the logisticians played a huge role in the sudden fall of Saddam's regime. John Keegan summed up their contributions when he wrote, "re-supply, quite as much as firepower or air support, was to be the secret of the coalition's overwhelming of Saddam's forces."[15]

When the logistical support system for the Tullahoma and Chickamauga campaigns are compared with the system used in the Iraq War, the similarities are striking. Major supply hubs were set up for funneling supplies into the area, Kuwait City and Louisville. Support organizations were responsible for gathering the supplies and forwarding them to the troops in the field, 377th TSC in Kuwait and COL Swords' officers and clerks in Louisville and Nashville. Forward logistical bases were used, Baghdad International Airport and Murfreesboro and Stevenson. Once the units left the port or railhead, they had to utilize more limited transportation assets to haul what they needed, assets that consumed resources even as they carried others forward, trucks and tankers and wagons with mule teams. The logistical units were set up at the same echelons of the armies in both conflicts: theater, army, corps, division, brigade, regiment-battalion. The final comparison is how logistical considerations drove the planning and operational tempo of the campaigns; without the means to move, feed, and arm the armies, the battles could never take place.

The study of logistics in past conflicts is most certainly relevant and can provide us insights even in this modern high-technological age. While the technology and equipment used today provides more options and flexibility in resupplying troops in the field, the principles that guide a logistical system have not changed: they are timeless. The same challenges faced by MG Rosecrans and his staff in 1863 were also faced by GEN Franks and his staff in 2003. By learning from the successes and failures of those who have come before us, the probability of our future success is greatly enhanced.

---

[1]David Jablonsky, *Roots of Strategy: Book 4* (Mechanicsburg, Pennsylvania: Stackpole Books, 1999), 76.

[2]Micheal DeLong, *Inside CENTCOM: The Unvarnished Truth about the Wars in Afghanistan and Iraq* (Washington, DC: Regnery Publishing, 2004), 6, 7, 20, 92.

[3]Ibid., 78-79, 91; and John Keegan, *The Iraq War* (New York: Alfred A. Knopf, 2004), 100, 136.

[4]Keegan, 132-135.

[5]377th Theater Support Command, "Operation Enduring Freedom and Iraqi Freedom Information Brief" (Fort Leavenworth, Kansas: Department of Logistics, US Army Command and General Staff College, April 2005).

[6]Keegan, 139, 141.

[7]Ibid., 147-149.

[8]David Zucchino, *Thunder Run: The Armored Strike into Baghdad* (New York: Atlantic Monthly Press, 2004), 68.

[9]DeLong, 105.

[10]Keegan, 154-157, 140.

[11]Ibid., 148-150.

[12]Zucchino, 86, 204, 223-224, 248, 256.

[13]Keegan, 163.

[14]377th TSC Brief

[15]Keegan, 146.

BIBLIOGRAPHY

Abdill, George B. *Civil War Railroads: A Pictorial Story of the War Between the States, 1861-1865*. Bloomington and Indianapolis, Indiana: Indiana University Press, 1961.

Alabama Historical Commission Marker. *Union Army Headquarters ("The Little Brick").* Stevenson, Alabama.

Biographical Sketch of Montgomery C. Meigs. Quartermaster Museum Homepage. Available from www.qmfound.com. Internet. Accessed on 10 December 2004.

Biographical Sketch of Thomas S. Jesup. Quartermaster Museum Homepage. Available from www.qmfound.com. Internet. Accessed 10 December 2004.

Bradley, Micheal R. *Tullahoma: The 1863 Campaign for the Control of Middle Tennessee.* Shippensburg, Pennsylvania: Burd Street Press, 2000.

Campaign Atlas of the Civil War. Department of History, United States Military Academy, 1980.

Carmicheal, Flossie, and Ronald Lee. *In and Around Bridgeport.* Collegedale, Tennessee: The College Press, 1967.

Catton, Bruce. *The Coming Fury.* New York, New York: Washington Square Press, 1967.

Connelly, Thomas L. *Civil War Tennessee: Battles and Leaders*. Knoxville, Tennessee: The University of Tennessee Press, 1979.

Cooper, William J. *Jefferson Davis, America.* New York: Alfred A. Knopf, 2000.

Cozzens, Peter. *The Battles for Chattanooga.* Fort Washington, Pennsylvania: Eastern National Park and Monument Association, 1996.

_________. *This Terrible Sound.* Urbana and Chicago, Illinois: University of Illinois Press, 1992.

Daniel, Larry J. *Days of Glory: The Army of the Cumberland, 1861-1865.* Baton Rouge, Louisiana: Louisiana State University Press, 2004.

Davis, George B., Leslie J. Perry, and Joseph W. Kirkley. *The Official Military Atlas of the Civil War.* Washington, D.C.: Government Printing Office, 1891.

Davis, John. "The Role of Ordnance Logistics in the Chickamauga Campaign." Master's thesis, US Army Command and General Staff College, Fort Leavenworth, Kansas, 1995.

DeLong, Micheal. *Inside CENTCOM: The Unvarnished Truth About the Wars in Afghanistan and Iraq.* Washington, D.C.: Regnery Publishing, 2004.

Department of the Cumberland-Department of the Tennessee. *Consolidated Monthly Inspection Reports of Cavalry, XIV, XX, XXI, Army Corps (1863).* Record Group 393, E-1063, Vol. 141, National Archives, Washington, D.C.

_________. *Monthly Inspection Reports Received (1863).* Record Group 393, Vols. 239-243, National Archives, Washington, D.C.

_________. *Monthly Inspection Reports--Cavalry and Batteries (1863).* Record Group 393, Vols. 239-243, National Archives, Washington, D.C.

Eisenhower, John S. D. *Agent of Destiny: The Life and Times of General Winfield Scott.* New York: The Free Press, 1997.

Engels, Donald W. *Alexander the Great and the Logistics of the Macedonian Army.* Berkeley and Los Angeles, California: University of California Press, 1978.

Foote, Shelby. *The Civil War: A Narrative--Fort Sumter to Perryville.* New York: Vintage Books, 1986.

Freemon, Frank R. *Gangrene and Glory: Medical Care during the American Civil War.* Urbana and Chicago, Illinois: University of Illinois Press, 2001.

Gabel, Christopher R. *Railroad Generalship: Foundations of Civil War Strategy.* Fort Leavenworth, Kansas: Combat Studies Institute, US Army, Command and General Staff College, 1997.

Gillett, Mary C. *The Medical Department: 1818-1865.* Washington, DC: Center of Military History, 1987.

Hagerman, Edward, *The American Civil War and the Origins of Modern Warfare: Ideas, Organization, and Field Command.* Bloomington and Indianapolis, Indiana: Indiana University Press, 1988.

Harbison, Robert E. "Wilder's Brigade in the Tullahoma and Chattanooga Campaigns of the American Civil War." Master's thesis, US Army Command and General Staff College, Fort Leavenworth, Kansas, 2002.

Hathaway, Richard J. *Michigan: Visions of Our Past.* East Lansing, Michigan: Michigan State University Press, 1989.

Huston, James A. *The Sinews of War: Army Logistics, 1775-1953*. Washington, DC: Office of the Chief of Military History, 1966.

Jablonsky, David. *Roots of Strategy: Book 4*. Mechanicsburg, Pennsylvania: Stackpole Books, 1999.

Keegan, John. *The Iraq War*. New York: Alfred A. Knopf, 2004.

Klein, Maury. *History of the Louisville & Nashville Railroad.* Lexington, Kentucky: The University of Kentucky Press, 2003.

Lamers, Wiliam M. *The Edge of Glory: A Biography of General William S. Rosecrans, U.S.A.* Baton Rouge, Louisiana: Louisiana State University Press.

Lee, Richard M. *Mr. Lincoln's City: An Illustrated Guide to the Civil War Sites of Washington.* McLean, Virginia: EPM Publications, 1981.

Longacre, Edward G. *Grant's Cavalryman: The Life and Wars of General James H. Wilson.* Mechanicsburg, Pennsylvania: Stackpole Books, 1972.

_________. *The Man behind the Guns: A Military Biography of General Henry J. Hunt, Chief of Artillery, Army of the Potomac.* Cambridge, Massachusetts: Da Capo Books, 2003.

McDonough, James Lee. *Stones River: Bloody Winter in Tennessee.* Knoxville, Tennessee: The University of Tennessee Press, 1980.

McPherson, James M. *Battle Cry of Freedom: The Civil War Era.* New York: Oxford University Press, 1988.

_________. *The Atlas of the Civil War.* New York: Macmillan, 1994.

Merrill, William E., COL. Tullahoma, Chickamauga, and Chattanooga Campaigns Military Map, 1865. Map for Chickamauga and Chattanooga, National Park Commission, printed in 1896.

Miller, David W. *Second Only to Grant: Quartermaster General Montgomery C. Meigs.* Shippensburg, Pennsylvania: White Mane Books, 2000.

Munden, Kenneth W., and Henry P. Beers. *The Union: A Guide to Federal Archives Relating to the Civil War.* Washington, D.C.: National Archives and Records Administration, 1986.

National Park Service Interpretive Marker. Crawfish Springs, Georgia, 2004.

Pagonis, William G. *Moving Mountains: Lessons in Leadership and Logistics from the Gulf War.* Boston, Massachusetts: Harvard Business School Press, 1992.

Pratt, Fletcher, *Stanton: Lincoln's Secretary of War.* Westport, Connecticut: Greenwood Press, 1953.

Prince, Richard E. *Nashville, Chattanooga and St. Louis Railway: History and Steam Locomotives.* Bloomington and Indianapolis, Indiana: Indiana University Press, 1967.

Richardson, Robert D. *Rosecrans' Staff at Chickamauga: The Significance of Major General William S. Rosecrans' Staff on the Outcome of the Chickamauga Campaign.* Master's thesis, US Army Command and General Staff College, Fort Leavenworth, Kansas 1989.

Risch, Erna,. *Quartermaster Support of the Army: A History of the Corps, 1775-1939.* Washington, D.C.: Quartermaster Historian's Office, 1962.

Robertson, John. *Michigan in the War.* Lansing, Michigan: W. S. George and Co. State Printers and Binders, 1882.

Robertson, William G., *The Battle of Chickamauga*, Fort Washington, Pennsylvania; Eastern National, 1995.

Rubenstein, David A. *A Study of the Medical Support to the Union and Confederate Armies During the Battle of Chickamauga: Lessons and Implications for Today's US Army Medical Department Leaders.* Master's thesis, US Army Command and General Staff College, Fort Leavenworth, Kansas, 1990.

Schrader, Charles R. *United States Army Logistics 1775-1992: An Anthology.* Vol. 1. Honolulu, Hawaii: University Press of the Pacific, 2001.

Shea, William L., and William L. Winschel. *Vicksburg Is the Key: The Struggle for the Mississippi River.* Lincoln, Nebraska: University of Nebraska, 2003.

Sheridan, Philip H. *The Personal Memoirs of P. H. Sheridan.* New York: DaLapo Press, 1992.

Starr, Paul. *The Social Transformation of American Medicine: The Rise of a Sovereign Profession and the Making of a Vast Industry.* United States: Basic Books, 1982.

Stevenson Depot Railroad Museum Board. *Historic Fort Harker.* Pamphlet, Stevenson, Alabama. Available from www.StevensonAlabama.com. Internet.

Stones River National Battlefield Informational Handout. *Stones River: Fortress Rosecrans.* National Park Service, US Department of the Interior, 2000.

Taylor, Lenette S. *The Supply for Tomorrow Must Not Fail: Civil War of Captain Simon Perkins Jr. a Union Quartermaster.* Kent, Ohio: The Kent State University Press, 2004.

Trefousse, Hans L. *Thaddeus Stevens: Nineteenth-Century Egalitarian.* Mechanicsburg, Pennsylvania: Stackpole Books, 2001.

Tucker, Glenn,. *Chickamauga: Bloody Battle in the West.* Dayton, Ohio: Morningside Bookshop, 1984.

Turner, George H. *Record of Service of the First Michigan Engineers and Mechanics in the Civil War, 1861-1865.* Kalamazoo, Michigan: Ihling Bros. and Everard for Adjutant General's Office, 1903.

US Army Command and General Staff College. Combat Studies Institute. "Staff Ride Information Handout on Logistics at Chickamauga." Fort Leavenworth, Kansas: Combat Studies Institute, US Army Command and General Staff College, 2004.

US Congress. House. *Annual Report of the Chief of Ordnance.* 38th Congress, Executive Documents. Washington, DC: Government Printing Office, 1863.

_________. *Annual Report of the Commissary General of Subsistence.* 38th Congress, Executive Documents. Washington, DC: Government Printing Office, 1864.

_________. House. *Annual Report of the Quartermaster General.* 38th Congress, Executive Documents. Washington, DC: Government Printing Office, 1863.

_________. House. *Annual Report of the Surgeon General.* 38th Congress, Executive Documents. Washington, DC: Government Printing Office, 1863.

US Department of the Army. Field Manual 4-0, *Combat Service Support.* Washington, DC: Department of the Army, August 2003.

US War Department. *The War of the Rebellion: A Compilation of the Official Records of the Union and Confederate Armies.* Series I. Vol. 23, part II. Washington, D.C. Government Printing Office, 1880-1901.

Van Creveld, Martin. *Supplying War.* Cambridge, United Kingdom: Cambridge University Press, 1977.

Weber, Thomas. *The Northern Railroads in the Civil War: 1861-1865.* Bloomington and Indianapolis, Indiana: Indiana University Press, 1952.

Webster's Ninth New Collegiate Dictionary. Springfield, Massachusetts: Merriam-Webster, 1988.

Widney, Lyman S., Diary 1863, Sergeant Major, 34th Illinois Infantry, Unit Files, Kennesaw Mountain National Military Park.

Woodhall, Eliza B. *The Stevenson Story.* Collegedale Tennessee: The College Press, Stevenson Depot Museum, 1982.

Woodworth, Steven E. *Six Armies in Tennessee: The Chickamauga and Chattanooga Campaigns.* Lincoln, Nebraska: University of Nebraska Press, 1998.

Yater, George H. *Two Hundred Years at the Falls of the Ohio: A History of Louisville and Jefferson County.* Louisville, Kentucky: The Heritage Corporation, 1979.

Zimmermann, Mark, *Guide to Civil War Nashville.* Nashville, Tennessee: Battle of Nashville Preservation Society, 2004.

Zucchino, David. *Thunder Run: the Armored Strike Into Baghdad.* New York: Atlantic Monthly Press, 2004.

377th Theater Support Command. "Operation Enduring Freedom and Iraqi Freedom Information Brief." Department of Logistics, US Army, Command and General Staff College, Fort Leavenworth, Kansas, April 2005.

CPSIA information can be obtained at www.ICGtesting.com
Printed in the USA
BVOW09s1812131016

464980BV00011B/81/P